Busine:

CW00540961

AAT Level 3 Diploma in Accounting

© Jo Osborne, 2022

All rights reserved. No part of this publication may be reproduced, stored in a retrieval system, or transmitted in any form or by any means, electronic, mechanical, photo-copying, recording or otherwise, without the prior consent of the copyright owners, or in accordance with the provisions of the Copyright, Designs and Patents Act 1988, or under the terms of any licence permitting limited copying issued by the Copyright Licensing Agency, Saffron House, 6-10 Kirby Street, London EC1N 8TS.

Image of owl © Eric Isselée-Fotolia.com

Published by Osborne Books Limited. Printed and bound by Stroma Ltd, UK.

Email books@osbornebooks.co.uk, Website www.osbornebooks.co.uk

ISBN 978-1-911198-94-9

how to use this Wise Guide

This Wise Guide has been designed to supplement your Tutorial and Workbook. It has two main aims:

■ to reinforce your learning as you study your course

■ to help you prepare for your online assessment

This Wise Guide is organised in the specific topic areas listed on pages 4 and 5. These individual topic areas have been designed to cover the main areas of study, concentrating on specific areas of difficulty. There is also an index at the back to help you find the areas you are studying or revising.

The Owl symbolises wisdom, and acts as your tutor, introducing and explaining topics. Please let us know if he is doing his job properly. If you have feedback on this material, please email books@osbornebooks.co.uk.

Thank you and good luck with your study and revision.

Osborne Books

REVISION TIPS

'OWL' stands for: Observe Write Learn

There are a number of well-known ways in which you can remember information:

- *You can remember what it looks like on the page. Diagrams, lists, mind-maps, colour coding for different types of information, all help you **observe** and remember.*

- *You can remember what you **write** down. Flash cards, post-it notes around the bathroom mirror, notes on a mobile phone all help. It is the process of writing which fixes the information in the brain.*

- *You can **learn** by using this Wise Guide. Read through each topic carefully and then prepare your own written version on flash cards, post-it notes, wall charts – anything that you can see regularly.*

- *Lastly, give yourself **chill out** time, your brain a chance to recover and the information time to sink in. Promise yourself treats when you have finished studying – a drink, chocolate, a work out. Relax! And pass.*

list of contents

1   Types of Business

HOW DIFFERENT BUSINESSES ARE STRUCTURED

Organisations can be structured in several different ways, all with different key characteristics depending on the type of business organisation, including the way they are set up and the legal framework they operate in.

The key types of business are:

Sole trader	an individual who owns and runs a business, and is completely responsible for it
Partnership (unlimited liability)	a number of individuals working together in business and sharing the profit (or losses)
Limited liability partnerships (LLP)	a number of individuals working together in business, sharing the profit (or losses), but with limited liability for the debts of the business

Limited partnerships	similar to an LLP except that only the general partner has unlimited liability
Public (plc) and private limited companies (ltd)	a limited company is a business owned by shareholders and run by directors (sometimes the same people). The liability of the shareholders is limited to the amount they have invested
Not-for-profit organisation	making profit is not the prime motive of these organisations. They include public sector organisations and charities

key features of a sole trader

- the owner is **independent**, and has **complete control** over how the business is run

- the business is easy to set up – either using the owner's name, or a trading name (which must not include ltd or plc)

- all profits made by the business belong to the owner

- the owner takes out profit as **drawings**

- the owner has **unlimited liability** for the losses and debts of the business – if the sole trader becomes insolvent, the owner's personal assets may be used to pay the business's debts

- the business is **funded by capital** – the owner can grow the business by introducing more capital, retaining and reinvesting profits, or by borrowing

- the owner often works long hours. If they take holidays or they are ill, the business will either slow down or stop completely until they return

- sole traders will normally produce a statement of profit or loss and a statement of financial position, although there is no required format for these

- a sole trader **must register with HMRC**, file an annual income tax return, and pay tax and national insurance on their profits. If they are VAT registered, they must also complete VAT returns

key features of a partnership (unlimited liability)

- all partners contribute **capital** to the partnership. Further capital can be raised by the introduction of new partners

- the profits of the business are shared based on the terms of the **partnership agreement**, and partners take their share as **drawings**

- the partnership must follow the rules of the **Partnership Act 1890**, and if there is no formal partnership agreement, profits must be split equally

- the partnership agreement also details other rights and responsibilities of the partners, such as salaries

- partnerships will build up **goodwill**; the difference between the value of a business and the net value of its assets and liabilities

- when a partner retires, or a new partner joins, goodwill must be calculated to work out the value of the retiring partner's share

- partners have **unlimited liability** for all the dealings and business debts of the whole partnership, not just their share

- decisions may take longer than for sole traders as more partners need to be consulted

- **individual partners may specialise** in particular areas of the business
- with several partners, there is cover for illness and holidays
- the retirement or death of one partner may adversely affect the running of the business
- a partnership **must register with HMRC**, and all partners are jointly responsible for filing an **annual tax return for the partnership**
- individual partners must also complete an annual self-assessment tax return

key features of a limited liability partnership

■ a limited liability partnership (**LLP**) is set up through **incorporation** at Companies House

■ although an LLP is a partnership, the owners of the business are called **members** not partners

■ the **members' liability is limited** to their investment in the business

■ a written or oral **members' agreement** sets out the rights, duties, and obligations of the members

■ all LLPs must have two or more '**designated members**' who are responsible for the legal and accounting requirements

■ the financial statements of an LLP are very similar to those of limited companies and comprise a statement of profit or loss, a statement of financial position, supporting notes, and an auditors' report (if applicable)

■ the LLP's confirmation statement and annual accounts must be filed at Companies House, where they are available for public inspection

key features of a limited partnership

- a limited partnership is **similar to an LLP** except that it must appoint at least one **general partner** and one **limited partner**

- all **limited partners will have limited liability**; however, the **general partner(s)' liability will be unlimited**

- the general partner is normally responsible for the day-to-day running of the business, with the limited partner, or partners, not taking an active role in the managerial decisions

- limited partnerships are often set up for projects that will last for a relatively short period of time, for which the limited partners are predominantly providing investment in return for a share of the returns

a limited company can be private, or a public limited company

	Private limited company (ltd)	Public limited company (plc)
Share capital	there is **no minimum** share capital, and shares **cannot** be sold to the public	the minimum issued share capital is **£50,000**, and shares **can** be traded on a stock exchange, and/or bought and sold by individuals, limited companies, and trusts
Shareholders	at least **one**	at least **two**
Directors	at least **one** which can be the same person as a sole shareholder	at least **two**

key features of limited companies

- a limited company is **incorporated** as a **separate legal** entity from its owners (shareholders)

- limited companies are **owned by shareholders** and **managed by directors**

- shareholders invest in the **share capital** of the company and are paid **dividends** out of the profits of the business

- limited companies must follow the rules and regulations of the **Companies Act 2006**, and must produce financial statements in accordance with Financial Reporting Standards (FRSs), or International Financial Reporting Standards (IFRSs)

- the articles of association set out the written rules for running the company that have been agreed by the shareholders, directors, and the company secretary

- the directors are responsible for submitting the company's annual confirmation statement and annual accounts to **Companies House**

- a company's annual accounts comprise:

  - statement of profit or loss

  - statement of financial position

- supporting notes to the financial statements (the depth of information required varies depending on the size of the company)
- directors' report to shareholders
- auditor's report (unless exempt from audit due to its size)

▧ the annual accounts are available for public inspection

advantages of incorporation	disadvantages of incorporation
• liability for members is limited to the amount they have invested	• more complex requirements for setting up the business
• the continuing existence of the business as a separate legal entity when ownership changes	• higher costs associated with record-keeping, maintaining documentation, and filing an annual return
• perceived as a more credible business – a limited company sounds more substantial than a sole trader	• business finances must be kept entirely separate from those of the owners
• more sources of finance available	• anyone can access financial and other information filed with Companies House

key features of not-for-profit organisations

- the motive of these organisations is not to make profit
- not-for-profit organisations include **public sector** organisations and **charities**

public sector organisations

- provide all public services in the UK, for example education, health, rubbish collection and recycling, and social care
- 'owned' by central and local **government** and funded by taxes
- public sector organisations sometimes form partnerships with private sector companies to provide a service, eg hospitals in the NHS
- the amount of money that public sector organisations have to spend on these services depends on the amount that is allocated to them in the budget

charities

- charities are set up to provide **charitable activities** within the scope of the charity

- most of their income is from donations, grants, and funding and most of their expenditure is finance for their charitable activities

- the key rules governing charities are set out in the **Charities Act 2011** and the Statement of Recommended Practice (SORP) Accounting and Reporting by charities, or FRS 102

- most charities are registered with **the Charity Commission**, the regulator for most charities

- charities are run by trustees and governed by a trust deed, which sets out the name of the charity, its objectives, and powers

- charities prepare an annual return which must be filed with the Charity Commission by the trustees and be available for public inspection

what are the common features of business organisations?

structure	a group of interrelated individuals, organised so that they can work together efficiently and effectively
common objectives and team working	defined objectives that will be achieved by individuals working together with **goal congruence**
co-operation	individuals must develop good working relationships, and work co-operatively, to achieve the organisation's goals
responsibility, authority, and division of work	individuals have defined responsibilities that identify what is expected of them and that divide the work between them. Authority will depend on the business structure and the individual's seniority

the difference between a manufacturing business and a service business?

manufacturing business
makes and sells tangible products, eg a bicycles manufacturer

service business
provides a service to individual customers or clients, or to another business, eg a delivery company

characteristics of a service business

intangibility	there is no physical product, ie the service cannot be seen, touched, tasted, or smelled
inseparability	the service cannot be separated from its consumption by the customer, ie it is usually consumed at the same time as it is provided
perishability	any unused service cannot be stored for future use
variability	a service will be tailored to the needs of an individual customer

2 Sources of funding

HOW DOES A BUSINESS FUND ITS OPERATIONS?

All organisations will need funds to operate. This may be to fund future growth, or to cover the costs of its day-to-day operations. There are various sources of funds available to businesses.

how to choose the right funding to use

Over the next couple of pages we will look at the different funding methods available to business organisations. When deciding what type of funding to use, a business must consider what the funding is to be used for, so that the appropriate method is selected.

Source of funding	What it is	What it's used for
Borrowing	Usually a bank loan The business will pay back the loan, plus interest, over an agreed period of time The repayment period should match the life of the asset it is being used to purchase	Longer term investment such as purchasing vehicles, buildings, assets
New capital	The business issues further share capital This can be purchased by existing shareholders or new shareholders This is a long term source of funds	Investment in business growth

Retained profit	Rather than distributing profit as dividends, a business retains the profits Shareholders must agree to this Shareholders will benefit if the business grows and the value of their investment increases	Investment in business growth
Working capital	The difference between the business's current assets and current liabilities cash + inventories + receivables – payables short term funding method	Day-to-day expenses of the business eg tax bill, paying suppliers, staff wages and bonuses

3 Business stakeholders

WHO ARE THE STAKEHOLDERS IN A BUSINESS?

A stakeholder is a person, or organisation, that has an interest in the business. Stakeholders are classified as either internal or external stakeholders.

Internal stakeholders	External stakeholders
Directors	Customers
Owners (shareholders)	Suppliers
Employees	Finance providers (banks)
	General public
	Professional and regulatory bodies
	Government

what do stakeholders require from the business?

stakeholder	requirements from the business
shareholders/owners	• generation of profit • return on investment • capital growth • dividends
directors	• appropriate remuneration • authority to make decisions • trust from the owners
employees	• fair pay • good working conditions • training and development • job security • career progression

customers	• good quality products or services at a fair price
	• support from the business if any issues arise
suppliers	• prompt payment to credit terms
	• loyalty
finance providers	• ability to make repayments
	• appropriate security for amounts borrowed
general public	• positive contribution to the local community
	• respect for the environment
professional or regulatory bodies	• compliance with regulations and standards
	• payment of subscriptions
government	• pay taxes
	• compliance with legislation
	• local and national employment

what do stakeholders contribute to the business?

stakeholder	contributions to the business
shareholders/owners	• capital investment • cooperation with directors
directors	• strong leadership • advocates for the business • loyalty
employees	• commitment to the business • strong work ethic and good attendance • pride in their work • loyalty
customers	• prompt payment to credit terms • brand loyalty

suppliers	• good quality products or services at a fair price
	• prompt delivery
	• support to the business if any issues arise
finance providers	• funds over an agreed period
general public	• support for business initiatives
professional or regulatory bodies	• the credibility of being a member of the professional or regulatory body
	• access to training and/or continuing professional development (CPD)
government	• fair rates of tax
	• clear legislation
	• financial support for businesses, where appropriate

4 Organisational structure and governance

HOW STRUCTURE AFFECTS THE WAY AN ORGANISATION OPERATES

The structure of an organisation and the span of control will have an impact on the way the organisation operates.

structure	examples
divisional: teams that focus on individual products, services, or geographical area	• firm of accountants, with teams for audit, accounting, taxation etc • multinational drinks company with divisions in UK, Europe, USA, and Australia
functional: organised into specialised functions or skills	• furniture manufacturer with sales, HR, finance, production, and despatch functions
matrix: staff work in departments, and also work across teams and projects	• engineering business with five product development teams, each with staff from finance production, sales, marketing and R&D

divisional structure

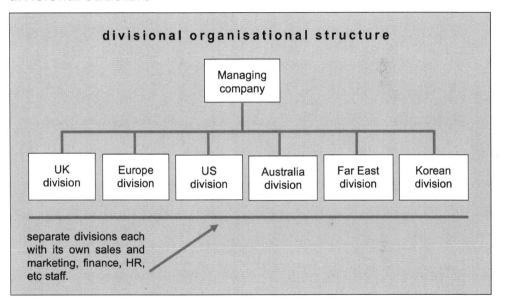

divisional organisational structure

Managing company

| UK division | Europe division | US division | Australia division | Far East division | Korean division |

separate divisions each with its own sales and marketing, finance, HR, etc staff.

functional structure

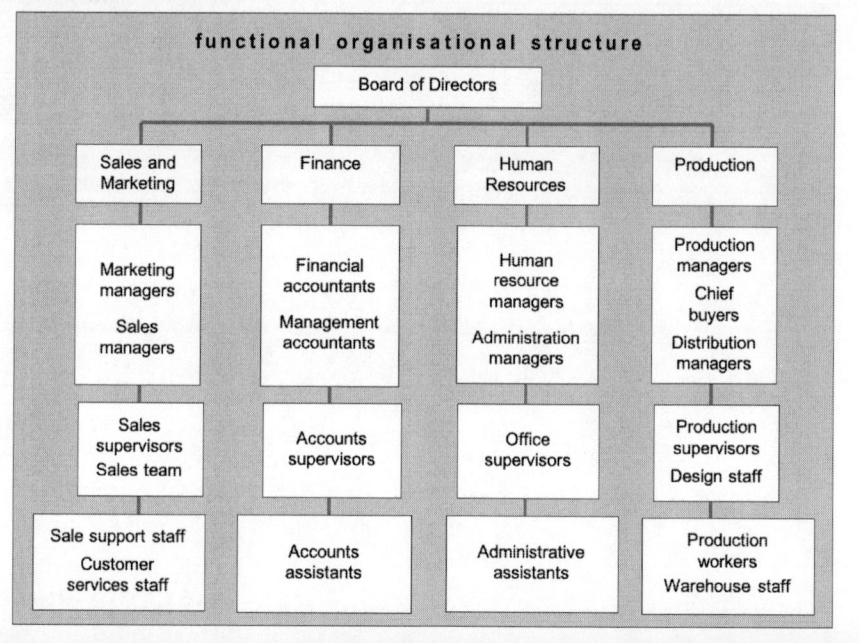

matrix structure

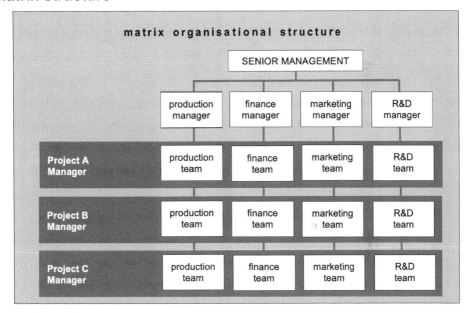

matrix organisational structure

SENIOR MANAGEMENT

	production manager	finance manager	marketing manager	R&D manager
Project A Manager	production team	finance team	marketing team	R&D team
Project B Manager	production team	finance team	marketing team	R&D team
Project C Manager	production team	finance team	marketing team	R&D team

span of control

Span of control is the number of individuals a manager is responsible for: the more people they manage, the wider their span of control. It also depends on:

■ **size of the organisation** – generally, managers in a smaller business will have a wider span of control

■ **type of work** that the individuals do – it is easier to manage a larger group of individuals that complete straightforward, repetitive tasks than a smaller group of individuals who carry out complicated task and diverse roles

■ **location of staff** – if all the individuals a manager is responsible for are physically located together, the span of control can be wider

The structure of a business can also been defined as a tall or a flat organisational structure.

A **tall organisational structure** has several layers of management with clear reporting lines. Managers have a narrow span of control, and decision-making takes longer as information must pass between multiple levels of management.

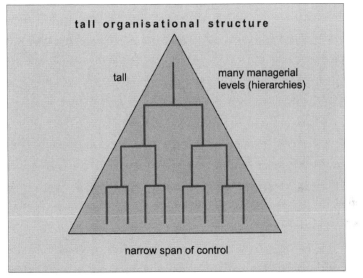

tall organisational structure

tall

many managerial levels (hierarchies)

narrow span of control

A **flat organisational structure** has fewer layers of management, meaning there is a wider span of control. Decisions can be made promptly and efficiently as information can pass up and down the chain of command quickly.

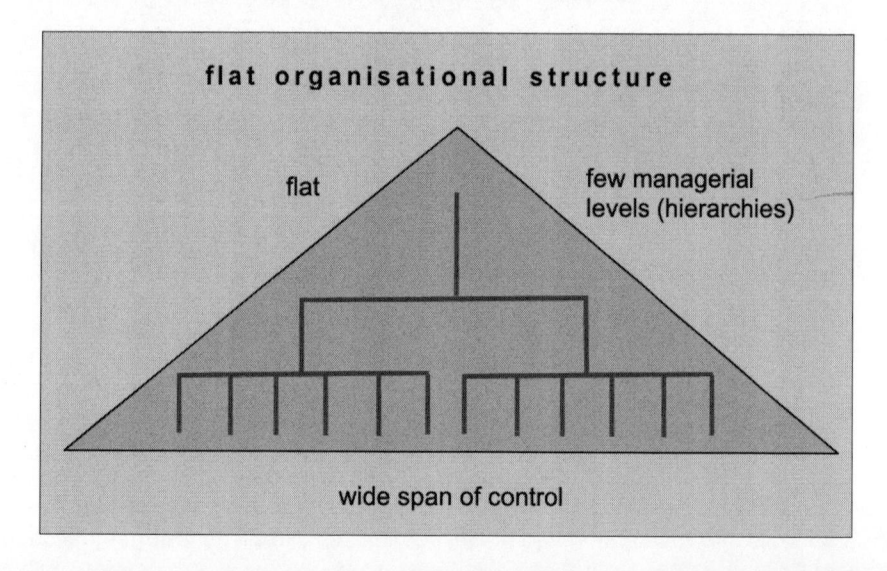

centralised and decentralised control

The extent to which control over decision-making is centralised is key to the way in which an organisation operates.

centralised control	decentralised control
• decisions made by more senior management levels	• authority for decision-making is given to lower management levels
• the more senior, the more influence an individual has	• leads to a more collaborative approach
• decisions are imposed on staff who are expected to implement them, ie a 'top-down' structure	• advantage – decisions can be made quickly
• less flexible, as staff do not contribute to decision-making	• disadvantage – lower level managers may not have the right experience to make the correct decision

governance

This is a system that provides a framework for managing organisations. It identifies who can make decisions, who has the authority to act on behalf of the organisation, and who is accountable for how the organisation and its people behave and perform.

Effective governance will include:

corporate governance:	systems that direct and control how the business is operated to achieve strategic objectives
financial governance:	systems for collecting, managing, and controlling financial information, and identifying financial risk
legal governance:	systems that ensure a business complies with the necessary legislation and regulation

levels of management

Different level of management in an organisation will be responsible for different types of decision making.

strategic/corporate level	• highest level of management • strategic decisions about the direction of the business and its goals • generally longer term decisions
managerial level	• middle level of management • decisions relating to the way the business will achieve its goals
operational level	• lowest level of management • decisions relating to the day-to-day operation of the business • generally short term decisions

working together

It is important that the different levels of management work together and support each other for the good of the organisation as a whole.

example:

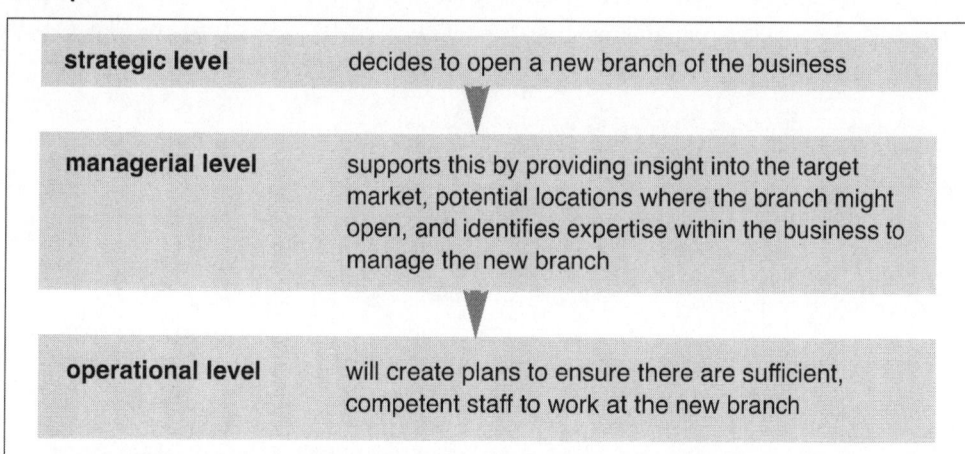

strategic level	decides to open a new branch of the business
managerial level	supports this by providing insight into the target market, potential locations where the branch might open, and identifies expertise within the business to manage the new branch
operational level	will create plans to ensure there are sufficient, competent staff to work at the new branch

5   Role of the finance function

HOW DOES THE FINANCE FUNCTION CONTRIBUTE TO THE OPERATION OF THE BUSINESS?

The finance function will interact with all the other functions in an organisation, providing information to each of them, and requiring information from them.

what are key functions of an organisation?

- **operations/production** — responsible for all activities involved in producing a product or providing a service

- **sales and marketing** — responsible for promoting and selling products and services

- **human resources** — responsible for managing and supporting the workforce, including recruitment, training, appraisal and pay

| **information technology** | responsible for setting up and maintaining all computer-based information systems, including websites, email systems, computer hardware, and software (including computerised accounting software) |
| **distribution and logistics** | responsible for receiving, storing and handling raw materials, and storing, distributing, and delivering finished products and services |

how does the finance function work with these functions?

operations/production	• **arranging credit with suppliers** – finance will manage the financial relationship with suppliers, including paying outstanding amounts
	• **inventory control** – monitoring inventory of raw materials and finished goods, and carrying out regular inventory counts
	• **budgeting** – setting and monitoring production budgets

sales and marketing	• **product pricing** – setting prices and establishing discount levels
	• **rates for services** – setting hourly rates for services eg accountancy staff charge-out rates, or the specific charge for a service, eg a cleaning contract
	• **budgeting** – setting and monitoring sales budgets
human resources (HR)	• **recruitment costs** – costs associated with recruiting staff must be factored into departmental and company cost budgets
	• **staff training and development** – HR must ensure staff receive appropriate training and development; finance must ensure the costs are included in the departmental budgets
	• **pay and benefits** – finance must budget for staff pay and benefits, and must receive details about pay rates and overtime rates etc to factor into the budget

information technology (IT)	• **investment in IT** – finance will carry out investment appraisal on new IT systems to ensure it is value for money
	• **data security** – IT and finance must ensure that data protection regulations are complied with
	• **KPIs** – IT will ensure that systems capture the correct financial and non-financial data to allow finance to set KPIs and monitor actual results against them
distribution and logistics	• **inventory management** – calculating reorder levels and lead times to ensure that there is sufficient inventory 'in the right place at the right time' for the business to operate
	• **exporting and importing** – providing advice on exchange rates and the tax implications of trading overseas
	• **KPIs** – setting KPIs and monitoring actual results against them

6   Risk and risk management

HOW DOES RISK AFFECT THE WAY A BUSINESS OPERATES?

*Risk can be defined as '**the possibility of something bad happening**.'
However, risk is not always a bad thing for a business – most business
decisions have an element of risk of failure. But if the decision proves to be a
good one then the risk has paid off.*

what is business risk?

Business risk is a business's vulnerability to factors that might decrease its profits or
even cause it to fail.

different types of business risk

Business risk can be analysed into different types of risk.

▓ **strategic risk**	risks arising from decisions that the directors make about the objectives (strategies) of the business
	example of a strategic risk would be a firm of accountants deciding to open a new office and then not attracting sufficient new clients to make it viable
▓ **financial risk**	risks resulting from a change in the financial conditions in which a business operates
	example of a financial risk would be a change in bank interest rates that increased the cost of a business loan
▓ **operational risk**	risks arising for the way in which an organisation operates its business functions. This could relate to the risk of failure of controls built into the business processes, loss of people who work for the business, failure in the systems used by the business, risks associated with failure to comply with legal and regulatory requirements, or event risks of something happening which is outside the control of the business
	example of an operational risk would be the risk of losing expertise if the production manager leaves the business

◼ **cyber risk**	risks arising from cyberattacks on a business's information systems
	examples of cyber risks are phishing, malware, ransomware, distributed denial-of-service attack (DDoS), spyware, keylogging, password attack and browser hijacking
	cyber risk is covered in more detail in chapter 19
◼ **reputational risk**	risk to the good name of a business, or its reputation. This may be due to the actions of the business, the actions of its employees, or the actions of a third party associated with it. Damage to its reputation can have an adverse effect on a business, and may result in lost sales, employees leaving, and a reluctance from suppliers, customers, and investors to continue to work with the business
	example of reputational risk would be a newspaper report identifying that the business does not pay a fair wage to its overseas workers

evaluating risk

So, once a business has identified risks, how does it manage these risks? Each risk should be assessed against:

- **likelihood** of the risk actually happening
- **impact** on the business if the risk actually does happen

Many businesses will use a **risk matrix** to evaluate risk. This is a table, or chart, that plots the impact on one axis, and likelihood on the other.

Impact				
4	4	8	12	16
3	3	6	9	12
2	2	4	6	8
1	1	2	3	4
	1	2	3	4
	Likelihood			

The risks with the highest grades will be the highest priority, ie high impact and high likelihood, whereas the lowest grade risks are less likely to be an issue.

managing risk

Once risks have been evaluated, they need to be managed. The **TARA framework** can be used to manage risk. TARA is a simple way or remembering the four possible actions that can be taken to address risk.

T transfer in certain situations the risk can be transferred to a third party

example: by insuring a factory, this would transfer the risk of loss due to fire or flood to the insurance company

A avoid a business may decide to avoid the risk completely by withdrawing from a situation, and should only really be considered when the risk is very likely to happen, and the impact would be significant

example: a business that operates in a country where there is a high risk of war may decide to withdraw its business from that country completely to avoid the impact of the war on its staff

R reduce taking steps to reduce the risk of something happening, and minimising the effect on the business if it does is normally the appropriate approach where the likelihood of a risk is high, but the impact is relatively low

example: a manufacturing business may choose to train its staff to ensure that the risk of high levels of waste in its production process is kept to a minimum

A accept in certain situations a business may decide to accept fact that a risk might happen, and deal with the consequences if it does; normally only when both the likelihood and impact of the risk are low

example: the organisers of the London marathon will have to accept the risk of rain on the day that the race is to be held

The TARA approach to managing risk can be plotted on a **risk map** like this:

		Impact/consequence on business	
Likelihood		**Low**	**High**
	High	Reduce the risk	Avoid the risk
	Low	Accept the risk	Transfer the risk

attitude to risk

Different businesses, and different stakeholders, will have varying attitudes to risk.

■ **risk averse**   keen to avoid risk, and so will go for option with lower risk

■ **risk seeking**   actively seeks out riskier options in the hope of higher returns

■ **risk neutral**   either falls somewhere between risk averse and risk seeking, or risk is not the primary factor in a decision

■ **risk appetite**   the level of risk someone is prepared to accept to achieve their objectives

■ **risk tolerance**   how much risk someone can withstand (tolerate); often measured as the financial loss that can be withstood

■ **risk threshold**   the level up to which risk is acceptable, this may be quantified as an amount of money that could be lost if a project fails

7 PESTLE analysis

HOW CAN A BUSINESS ANALYSE THE EXTERNAL FACTORS THAT MAY AFFECT IT?

PESTLE analysis can be used to analysis external factors.

P	Political
E	Economic
S	Social
T	Technological
L	Legal
E	Environmental

PESTLE analysis allows businesses to assess external factors, and to identify ways in which it can adapt to minimise risks and maximise opportunities.

political factors

These factors relate to the extent the Government influences the economy. Political factors include:

- **government policy** – for example, the Government's attitude to overseas investment in businesses in this country, or the policies of overseas governments to foreign businesses operating in their country
- **taxation** – the Government sets the tax rates. An increase in corporation tax rates will have an adverse effect on a business's profit, an increase in VAT rates will increase the prices paid by consumers, and an increase in income tax rates will reduce disposable income of consumers. Decreases in any of these will have the opposite effect
- **import and exports** – governments may impose tariffs on imports and exports. UK import tariffs protect domestic businesses from being 'undercut' by cheaper imports. Similarly, businesses that export may be faced with tariffs in the countries to which they export
- **public spending** – expenditure in the public sector is known as public spending. The Government collects taxes and decides where to spend them, which impacts businesses that provide goods and services to the public sector

economic factors

The financial state of the UK economy, and sometimes the global economy, is a key factor that affects consumer demand, growth of a business, and its profitability. Economic factors include:

- **interest rates** – increases in interest rates will make borrowing more expensive for businesses and individuals. They will also reduce consumer spending as those with debt will have higher interest costs, and those with available funds will save more. Decreases in interest rates will have the opposite effect

- **exchange rates** – the value of one currency when it is converted into another, eg £1: US$1.35. A fall in the exchange rates, ie a weak £, means exports from the UK will be cheaper for overseas buyers and imports will be more expensive for UK businesses. A strong £ will have the opposite effect – overseas buyers will pay more, but UK businesses that import will pay less

■ **inflation** – this is the percentage rise in prices over time. Businesses do not want high levels of inflation as this will cause rapid price increases and discourage customer spending

demand-pull inflation	when demand for products and services increases, and businesses cannot meet the demand, prices rise
cost-push inflation	when the supply of goods and services decreases because production costs have increased

■ **disposable income** – the amount people have to spend after taxes and essential living costs have been paid. When the economy is growing, and unemployment levels are low, disposable income will rise, leading to higher levels of spending. When economic growth decreases, individuals' income reduces and spending on good and services will reduce

■ **business cycles** – the level of production of goods and services does not stay constant. Fluctuations in the economy are known as the business cycle (sometimes the economic or trade cycle). The four elements of the business cycle are:

boom   an upturn in the economy where unemployment is low and consumer demand is high

downturn   eventually the boom phase will come to an end and inflation and interest rates will start to rise, making businesses more cautious, and causing the economy to slow down

recession   if the economy slows down so much that it actually shrinks for two successive quarters, this is known as a recession

recovery   after a period of recession, the Government will try and stimulate the economy by lowering interest rates, prompting businesses to invest and grow, leading to the creation of more jobs and an increase disposable income

social factors

These factors relate to the society in which a business operates. This can be local, national, or international. Social factors include:

- **demographic factors** such as income levels, employment levels, language and culture, religion, education levels, family structures, age, and occupations. Businesses must monitor demographic changes to ensure their products and services remain relevant to the society in which they operate

- **trends** – businesses must also monitor trends and changing tastes, to ensure that they adapt their products and services to remain relevant and competitive

- **unemployment** – higher levels of unemployment may mean there is a larger population for a business to obtain its workforce from. High local unemployment will mean that disposable income will be lower, so businesses such as supermarkets may have to consider selling more basic ranges, or differentiating their prices in certain areas to attract customers

technological factors

These factors relate to the way **changes in technology** can have a positive or negative impact on how a business operates and its structure.

Examples of the **positive impact** of technology are:

- easier access to market through website sales and internet marketing
- computer aided design (CAD) reducing the time it takes between an idea for a product and production
- automated production lines reducing labour costs and increasing productivity
- improved safety due to automation of processes
- electronic point of sales systems (EPOS) which monitor inventory from the warehouse to the checkout, and provide instant up-to-date data on inventory levels and consumer spending habits
- more choice for consumers and information on products via the internet
- global communication allowing businesses to relocate support departments overseas to reduce costs

■ Businesses may decide to outsource elements of their production processes to other business in the UK, or overseas. Technology allows them to remotely monitor production, which reduces the risk of quality issues and/or delays in supply previously associated with outsourcing

Examples of the **negative impact** of technology are:

■ products becoming obsolete more quickly, meaning inventory of older versions needs to be sold more cheaply, or written off

■ more choice for consumers and more information on products via the internet meaning they can easily switch from one supplier to another

■ the introduction of automated processes may result in staff redundancies, costing the business money and causing staff unrest

legal factors

Businesses must ensure that they comply with laws and regulations, and keep up-to-date with changes when they happen. Examples of legal factors are:

- **national minimum wage regulations** – businesses must ensure that they pay employees in accordance with the national minimum wage regulations in the UK. Business must also ensure they pay overseas workers a fair wage

- **health and safety law** – particularly relevant to production businesses, this legislation is designed to keep the workforce safe

- **employment law** – legislation that ensures employees are treated fairly; it includes rights to maternity/paternity leave and flexible working

- **discrimination law** – the Equality Act (2010) protects employees against discrimination, eg age, disability, sex, race, religion, and pregnancy

- **consumer protection** – eg clear labelling of products and services so that consumers know what they are buying

- **import/export law** – businesses must comply with UK and overseas laws and tariffs

environmental factors

These factors relate to the effect the environment has on the business. Environmental factors create two types of issue for businesses:

■ **the impact of environmental change** – the business needs to adapt the way it operates to deal with this. This may be:

  – availability of non-renewable resources such as oil and gas making businesses change the way goods are transported

  – climate change affecting farming methods

  – increased pollution

■ **the need to act sustainably** – business must act to protect the resources of the planet. Factors affecting a business's attitude to sustainability may be:

  – businesses may be motivated to protect the environment

  – the Government may introduce legislation that protects the environment and requires businesses to act sustainably

  – customer expectations that a business is 'green', ie environmentally friendly, may drive sustainability

example of a PESTLE Analysis

Issue	Action
Political The business sells luxury products. An increase in taxation has reduced disposable income.	Investigate selling other products that are not luxury items to maintain sales levels.
Economic The business imports raw materials. Fluctuating exchange rates make it difficult to predict the actual price that will be paid.	Negotiate prices with overseas suppliers in UK £s.
Social The business produces traditional designs, whereas customers tastes have changed, and they now want more modern designs.	Develop new ranges with more modern designs.

Technological	
Customers cannot buy directly from the business's website, leading to lost sales.	Update the website so that customers can buy directly.
Legal	
The Government has introduced legislation requiring businesses to use recycled packing for all goods.	Replace package material with recycled packing.
Environmental	
The business imports raw materials which are air freighted to the UK. These are raw materials that are available in the UK.	Consider purchasing the raw materials from UK suppliers.

ECONOMIC FACTORS THAT AFFECT ORGANISATIONS

Supply and demand, competition, and the effects of barriers to entry to the market are all micro-economic factors that affect the way a business operates.

concept of supply and demand

The price that a consumer is charged for a good or service is determined by supply (how much is available), and demand (how much consumers want). The laws of supply and demand will operate separately and interact to arrive at the market price.

demand	supply
the quantity consumers are willing and able to buy at different prices	the quantity sellers are prepared to offer for sale at different prices

demand – the nature of goods and services will affect how demand changes when income rises and falls.

- ▨ **normal goods**   demand for these goods goes up as income rises, and down as it falls

- ▨ **inferior goods**   demand decreases as income rises. People can afford these goods when income is lower, but when income rises, they chose more expensive alternatives, eg own brand baked beans might be an inferior good

- ▨ **necessity goods**   certain goods, such as medicines, water, and power, are a necessity. So demand for these products is less sensitive to changes in income or price

- ▨ **substitute goods**   two, or more, goods that carry out the same purpose for the consumer. If the price of one rises, this will increase demand for the other, and vice versa

- ▨ **complementary goods**   goods that must be used together, eg a games console and games. The rise in the price of one will cause a fall in demand for the other, and vice versa

demand curve

- ▧ for most products, demand increases (expands) as the price falls, and decreases (contracts) as the price rises

- ▧ this relationship can be plotted on a demand curve, like this one

- ▧ demand curves will always curve down

- ▧ price is on the vertical axis, quantity on the horizontal axis, and D is demand

- ▧ if the price falls from P1 to P2, demand rises from Q1 to Q2

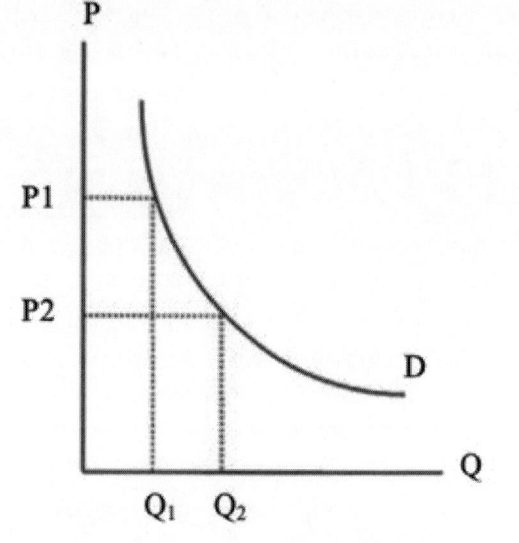

shift along the demand curve and shift in the demand curve

- a change in price will result in a move **along the demand curve**. If the price goes up, demand goes down. If the price goes down, demand goes up

- an increase in demand for a good or service, at the same price – maybe an influencer on social media uses the product in their content – results in the whole **demand curve shifting to the right**

- a decrease in demand for a good or service – maybe if the price of a substitute product has gone down – results in the whole **demand curve shifting to the left**

supply curve

- for most products, supply increases as the price rises, and falls when the price falls – suppliers will be keen to sell more if the price increases

- this relationship can be plotted on a supply curve, like this one

- supply curves always slope up

- price is on the vertical axis, quantity on the horizontal axis, and S is demand

- if the price increases from P2 to P1, quantity rises from Q2 to Q1

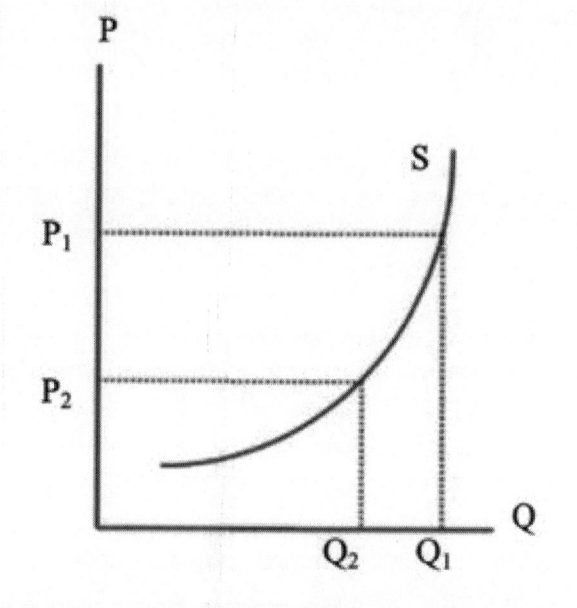

shift along the supply curve and shift in the supply curve

▓ a change in price will result in a move **along the supply curve**. If the price goes up, quantity goes up. If the price goes down, quantity goes down

▓ if something other than price affects supply, this will cause a shift in the whole supply curve. If supply is reduced – maybe due to the scarcity of raw materials – this results in the whole **supply curve shifting to the left**

▓ if the cost of production reduces so more goods can be produced at the same price – maybe because a production line has been automated – this results in the **supply curve shifting to the right**

the price mechanism

- generally, consumers want to pay the lowest price possible, and suppliers want to charge as much as possible

- there will have to be a compromise between the two where supply and demand are equal

- this doesn't happen instantly, but once supply and demand have adjusted, the **equilibrium price** will be reached (where the supply and demand curves bisect)

- the market forces of supply and demand have found a **price mechanism**, to determine the price of goods

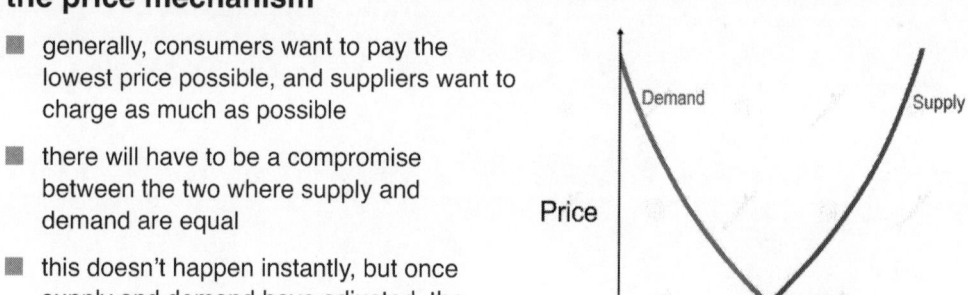

competition

There are a number of factors that affect competition in the market.

- **product features** – the more a supplier can **differentiate** its product, the fewer competitors it will have

- **number of buyers and sellers** – the more sellers in the market, the more choice consumers have, and the more competitive it will be. More buyers means suppliers must be more competitive

- **barriers to entry** – these are costs, or obstacles, that stop, or put off, new suppliers from entering the market. These include:

    - **legal barriers** such as licences trade standards and regulations

    - high **set-up costs**, such as investment in property or equipment

    - **brand loyalty** to other established products in the market

    - particular **expertise** maybe required which is scarce and/or expensive

- **availability of information** – if information about different suppliers is readily available, this means that competition increases

9 Sustainability

WHAT IS SUSTAINABILITY?

Sustainability has become increasingly important over recent years, with increased emphasis on 'green' policies. But sustainability goes beyond simply being environmentally friendly.

The three aspects of sustainable performance are:

- *economic/financial growth*
- *ecological/environmental*
- *social*

a definition of sustainability

The Brundtland commission defined sustainability as:

'development that meets the needs of the present without compromising the ability of future generations to meet their own needs.'

The key here is for businesses to take a longer-term view rather than focusing on 'profit at all costs.'

the triple bottom line

The three aspects of sustainable performance are sometimes referred to as the **triple bottom line**.

Economic growth, environmental protection and social equality may also be abbreviated to '**profit, planet and people**'.

economic growth and sustainability

Sustainable development requires resources to make it happen, **economic growth** provides these resources. Specifically:

- ▧ individual countries – economic growth of country should lead to an increase in that country's wealth which then benefits its population as a whole
- ▧ individual organisations – profit generated by organisations will increase the wealth of the owners and employees

Economic growth should not be pursued at the expense of social or environmental sustainability.

environmental protection and sustainability

Protection of the environment is key to conserving the world's resources, with organisations keen to highlight their 'green' credentials. You may have heard the phrase **'reduce, re-use, recycle'**. Some examples of environmentally friendly policies that contribute to sustainability are:

- supermarkets are required to charge customers for plastic shopping bags to reduce the number of plastic bags that end up in landfill

- recycling paper, metal, and certain plastics

- using recycled raw material and office supplies

- using low-emission, or electric, vehicles

- holding online meetings that reduce flights, driving or train travel

- only trading with suppliers that have certified green policies

The main objective of 'green' policies is to protect the environment, but a business may also save money by using less energy and other consumables.

social equality and sustainability

Sustainability must also focus on the social well-being of people. This may be:

■ ensuring that employees are happy and treated well in the workplace

■ considering the social equality of the local community

■ considering social equality of society as a whole

Organisations can promote social responsibility locally and worldwide in various ways. For example:

■ charitable donations which help and support the socially underprivileged

■ trading with overseas suppliers that provide reasonable pay and decent working conditions for their staff

■ supporting local initiatives to get out of work people back into the workplace

■ sponsoring local sports events that 'give back' to the local community

■ allowing staff to volunteer in community-based projects during work time

corporate social responsibility (CSR)

CSR means that businesses play a positive role in society and consider the environmental and social impact of decisions that they make.

Many businesses publish a **corporate social responsibility (CSR) report**, setting out the steps they are taking to support sustainable development. A CSR report also identifies to what extent it has achieved its CSR objectives.

There is **no legal requirement** to publish a CSR report, but organisations have realised that the public and investors want to know about their attitude to sustainability.

Organisations that can show progress towards achieving their CSR goals will enhance their reputation as an ethical organisation.

A CSR report should strike the right balance of positive and negative information. Too positive and it may look like a public relations exercise!

responsibility of accountants to uphold sustainability

Accountants are expected to uphold sustainability at the practice they work for and its clients, or in the business that they are employed by.

Professional accountants have to protect society as a whole,

■ ensuring the long-term responsible management of resources used by their organisation

■ contributing to the running of their organisation in a sustainable manner

■ assessing and minimising the risks to the organisation, and to society as a whole, of not acting sustainably

the needs of wider stakeholders

Accountants produce a significant amount of information that will be used by a wide range of stakeholders. This will include information about the organisation's sustainability credentials. The accountant's ethical duty of integrity means that when preparing this information, they must be transparent, ie not hide anything, and must ensure that this information is not misleading to its potential users.

promoting sustainability

Accountants must promote sustainable practices throughout the organisation in relation to each of the following:

▦ **products and services**   *example: ensuring that the products or services supplied by the organisation are produced from sustainably resourced materials, and that suppliers' staff have fair pay and decent working conditions*

▦ **customers**   *example: businesses should supply their customers in a sustainable manner, through efficient delivery methods, and fair long-term pricing strategies*

▦ **employees**   *example: encouraging staff to take appropriate qualifications, and providing them with good working conditions*

▦ **the workplace**   *example: implementing green policies relating to recycling and conservation of energy and then monitoring the participation of staff in the schemes as a measure of their success*

▨ **the supply chain**	*example: encouraging their organisation or clients to source supplies from suppliers with an ethical approach to sustainability*
▨ **business functions and processes**	*example: constantly reviewing the way in which the business operates to ensure that it continues to be responsible and supports and encourages sustainability and sustainable development*

10 Principles of professional ethics

WHAT ARE ETHICS?

Ethics can be defined as:

'the moral principles or standards that govern the conduct of the members of an organisation.'

Accountants are expected to maintain the standards of the organisation that they work for, or the professional accounting body to which they belong. As part of this they are expected to behave in a professional and ethical manner.

AAT code of professional ethics

AAT's **code of professional ethics** is based on the International Ethics Standards Board for Accountants (IESBA)'s Code of Ethics.

Compliance with the ethical code is a **professional obligation** rather than a legal obligation.

The Code is designed to help AAT members with ethical decisions.

Specifically, it:

- sets out the expected standard of professional behaviour

- helps protect the public interest

- helps to maintain AAT's good reputation

It is important to know that the AAT code of professional ethics applies to all fellow, full, affiliate and student members of AAT.

the fundamental ethical principles

A professional accountant is required to comply with the five fundamental principles.

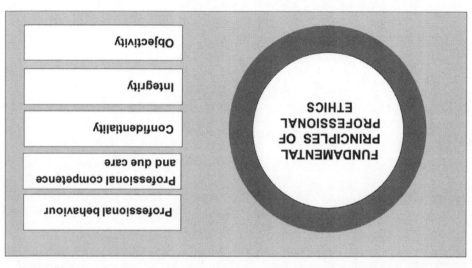

FUNDAMENTAL PRINCIPLES OF PROFESSIONAL ETHICS

- Professional behaviour
- Professional competence and due care
- Confidentiality
- Integrity
- Objectivity

integrity

Accountants should be **straightforward and honest** in their work.

Failing to act with integrity may mean that the accountant is directly or indirectly associated with misleading information, leading to users of the information such as clients, colleagues, or even the general public, no longer trusting the accountant, or the accountancy professional as a whole.

There are three key ethical values associated with integrity:

- **honesty**   being truthful and trustworthy

- **transparency**   operating in a way that makes it easy for others to see what is being done or said

- **fairness**   acting reasonably, and without bias

A professional accountant must ensure at all times that they act with integrity, honesty, transparency, and fairness whether they are dealing with clients, suppliers, or colleagues.

objectivity

An accountant must not allow bias, conflict of interest or undue influence from others, override their professional or business judgement.

- **conflicts of interest** – arise if the business or personal interests of an accountant could influence them giving an objective opinion. To remain objective, accountants must ensure that any conflict of interest is resolved as soon as it arises

- **independence** – accountants must not be influenced by pressure from others, including colleagues, clients, family, or friends. They must remain independent, only considering points that are relevant to decisions they must make, or work to be carried out, so that they protect their objectivity

- **appearing objective** – as well as being independent and objective, accountants must also be **seen to be objective**. This means ensuring that a third party would be confident that their actions appear to be objective and free from the influence of others

professional competence and due care

An accountant must **maintain the professional knowledge and skills** they need to carry out their work competently, to the required standard.

Accountants will maintain their professional competence through:

- **professional qualifications** – qualifying as a professional accountant means that they will have demonstrated a required level of skill and ability

- **continuing professional development (CPD)** – professional accounting bodies expect their members to stay up-to-date by carrying out regular CPD through reading current information on technical developments in the profession, or attending relevant training courses. Failure to carry out CPD may result in disciplinary action by the accountant's professional body

Accountants must also carry out their work with **due care**. This means carrying out their work carefully, thoroughly, and in the appropriate amount of time.

If an accountant does not have the necessary skills to competently carry out the work allocated to them, or enough time to do it with sufficient care, they should raise this with someone more senior in the organisation and/or ask for help.

confidentiality

Accountants have a **duty of confidentiality**. This means they must respect the confidentiality of information about a client or employer that has been gained during their employment, or during the course of their professional work.

This duty of confidentiality applies whilst the accountant works for an employer or client, but then also **extends after the working relationship** has ended.

■ **Disclosure of confidential information** – there are certain situations when confidential information can be disclosed

- a **client may authorise their accountant to disclose confidential information** if they are asked for a refence by a supplier, or a customer, of the client, or by their bank. The important thing is that the accountant must get permission from the client to disclose the information

- **disclosure of confidential information required by law** will be:
  - where it is required as evidence in court
  - where the law has been broken, and the information needs to be disclosed to the relevant authorities. A good example of this is money laundering which is covered in chapter 16

- there are also certain circumstances where an accountant will have a **professional duty to disclose confidential information**. This kind of disclosure can be a complex decision, so if they are in any doubt, the accountant should seek professional or legal advice before disclosing any information

professional behaviour

The AAT code of ethics says that accountants should:

'adopt professional behaviour to comply with relevant laws and regulations and avoid any action that brings our profession into disrepute'

Accountants must ensure that their behaviour, both inside and outside their workplace, does not reflect badly on the accountancy profession, or their professional accounting body.

- an accountant who fails to comply with accounting standards, or relevant laws and regulations, or knowingly gives misleading professional advice, will damage their own reputation and also the reputation of the accountancy profession

- an accountant who behaves badly outside work, for example getting involved in violence at a football match, would also be considered to be behaving unprofessionally, even thought they were not actually working. The very fact that they are an accountant and are behaving this way will inevitably reflect badly on the accounting profession

internal disciplinary procedures by an employer

If an accountant does not maintain the standard of professional behaviour expected of them, their employer may bring disciplinary procedures against them. These disciplinary procedures will normally include some, or all, of the following stages:

- verbal warning

- written warning

- disciplinary hearing

- opportunity to appeal

- suspension from work

- dismissal

The extent of the disciplinary action taken will depend on how bad the behaviour was. Theft or fraud would result in the accountant being dismissed, whereas posting a harmless joke on social media may only result in a verbal warning if it is the first time it has happened.

disciplinary action by professional accounting bodies

UK **professional accounting bodies** expect their members to comply with their codes of ethics, and to uphold the high standards of the accounting profession.

Disciplinary action against an accountant by their professional accounting body will involve an investigation, followed by a decision as to whether the accountant is guilty of misconduct.

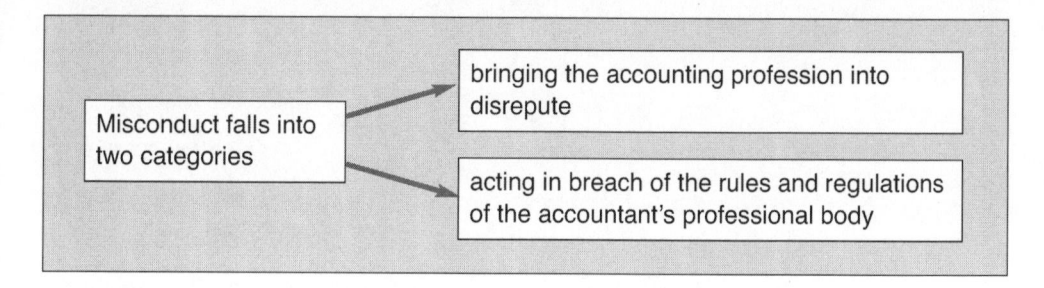

Misconduct falls into two categories

- bringing the accounting profession into disrepute
- acting in breach of the rules and regulations of the accountant's professional body

Depending on the severity of the misconduct, the accountant could face any of the following penalties:

- being required to provide written confirmation they will stop the misconduct and will not repeat it again
- being issued with a fine
- being declared ineligible for a practicing licence
- having their practicing licence withdrawn
- having their membership to the accounting body suspended
- being expelled from the professional accounting body

11 Professional scepticism, fraud and bribery

ACCOUNTANTS SHOULD BE SCEPTICAL

Accountants must ensure that they exercise professional scepticism when making professional judgements, particularly in relation to the recording of transactions, and financial reporting.

what is professional scepticism?

Professional scepticism is an attitude that includes:

- a questioning mind, ie not taking what is said at face value
- being alert to the possibility of misstatement due to error or fraud, and using professional experience to identify signs of genuine errors or deliberate fraud
- critically assessing evidence that is provided

Don't assume everything you are told is fraudulent	**Do** investigate further if an explanation is vague, or there is insufficient information

fraud

UK law defines fraud as:

'making a dishonest representation for your own advantage or to cause another a loss, or dishonestly neglecting to disclose information when you had a duty to do so.'

The **Fraud Act 2006** includes three classes of fraud:

■ fraud by false representation – saying or doing something you know is misleading

■ fraud by failing to disclose information – failing to disclose information you have a legal duty to disclose

■ fraud by abuse of position – abusing a position of trust where you are expected to safeguard the financial interest of another person

An accountant must be vigilant to the possibility of fraudulent behaviour by a client or colleague. They must ensure that their own objectivity is not compromised, to avoid any accusations of fraud.

bribery

A definition of **bribery** is:

'giving or receiving something of value with the intention of influencing the recipient to do something favourable to the giver of the bribe.'

The **Bribery Act 2010** covers the criminal law relating to bribery. The four key offences are:

- bribing another
- receiving a bribe
- bribing a foreign official
- failing to prevent bribery

The maximum penalty for someone found guilty of bribery is 10 years imprisonment and/or an unlimited fine, and their property can also be confiscated.

Again, an accountant must ensure that their objectivity is not compromised, for example by the accepting of gifts from a client, as this could lead to accusations of bribery.

12 Threats and safeguards to ethical principles

THREATS AND SAFEGUARDS

In some situations an accountant's ethical principles may be threatened. It is important that these threats are identified quickly, and safeguards are put in place to eliminate them or reduce them to an acceptable level.

taking a principles-based approach

The AAT code of ethics says that accountants should take a principles-based approach to ethics. But what does this mean?

- a principles-based approach means identifying, evaluating, and addressing threats to their compliance with the fundamental principles

- accountants should evaluate anything that may prevent them following the fundamental ethical principles

- because the accountant must evaluate each individual situation, there is less chance of someone finding loopholes that will excuse unethical behaviour

types of threats

Potential threats to an accountant's fundamental ethical principles fall into the following categories:

self-interest threat	a financial or other interest may influence the accountant's judgement or behaviour
self-review threat	an accountant has to re-evaluate a judgement they have previously made, or work they have carried out
familiarity threat	a close personal relationship causes the accountant to be too sympathetic to the interests of another
intimidation threat	an accountant is deterred from acting objectively because of a real or perceived threat from another person
advocacy threat	an accountant promotes a position or opinion (normally of a client) to the point that their objectivity may be compromised in the future

examples of self-interest threats

- direct or indirect financial interest in a client or employer

- loans to or from a client or employer

- a financial interest in a joint venture with a client or employee(s) of a client

- fees from a client representing a large proportion of total gross fees

- concern about the financial impact of losing a client

- potential employment with a client

- finding a significant error when reviewing previous work carried out by the accountant themselves, or a member of their staff

- concern for an accountant in business over their job security

- a financial interest in the business, eg performance-related bonus

examples of self-review threats

- accountant who used to work in practice now works for a client and has to review work they previously carried out

- accountant who used to work for a client now works in practice and has to review work they previously carried out

- accountant finds a significant error when reviewing work they have previously carried out and is concerned about the implications

- accountant is asked to report on the operation of financial systems after being involved in the design and implementation of these systems

- accountant in business is involved in the preparation of data for business decisions that the accountant will also be involved in taking

examples of familiarity threats

◼ accountant has a close or personal relationship with the client, or a key member of the client's staff. This may have a negative effect on the objectivity and the independence of the accountant

◼ accountant who was formerly a partner in the accounting practice is now a director, officer, or employee at the client, and has significant influence over the work the accounting practice carries out for the client

◼ accountant is offered gifts or preferential treatment by a client

◼ a long association between a senior member of the accountancy team and the client

◼ a close family relationship between an accountant in business and a supplier, customer, work colleague or manager

examples of intimidation threats

- client threatening to dismiss the accountant

- client threatening not to award a contract to the accountant

- threat of litigation by a client

- pressure to reduce the quality of work in order to reduce fees

- threat of dismissal by an employer

- a dominant person attempting to influence the decision-making process by making their point too forcefully

examples of advocacy threats

- accountant promoting a client's position by actively supporting the client or speaking on their behalf

- working on behalf of a client in a legal case, or in a dispute with another third party, eg a supplier, customer or competitor

- promoting shares in a listed business when the business is an audit client

summary of the threats likely to be made to each of the fundamental ethical principles

Threat / Principle	Self-interest threat	Familiarity threat	Intimidation threat	Self-review threat	Advocacy threat
Integrity	✔	✔	✔		
Objectivity	✔	✔	✔	✔	✔
Professional behaviour	✔	✔		✔	
Professional competence and due care	✔	✔		✔	
Confidentiality	✔	✔	✔		

safeguards against threats to fundamental ethical principles

How does an accountant deal with threats to their fundamental ethical principles?

If a threat has been identified, appropriate **safeguards** need to be in place to **eliminate the threat or reduce it to an acceptable level**.

Many of the safeguards will be included in **documented organisational policies** including:

- requirement to comply with the fundamental principles

- appropriate disciplinary processes to promote compliance

- procedures that identify interests or relationships between staff, or with clients

- procedures that encourage and empower staff to communicate concerns to senior members of staff

- requirement for staff to carry out sufficient, relevant CPD

- procedures to implement and monitor the quality of training

There should also be:

- strong leadership that stresses the importance of ethical behaviour and the expectation that employees will act in an ethical manner

- recruitment procedures that emphasise the importance of employing high calibre, competent staff

- the opportunity to ask advice from other appropriate professional members of staff

- the requirement to comply with professional accounting standards

- policies and procedures that encourage employees to communicate any ethical issues to senior management without fear of retribution

what if safeguards are not sufficient?

If a threat cannot be eliminated or reduced to an acceptable level, even if safeguards are put in place, the accountant must refuse to accept, or continue with, the work they are being asked to complete.

13 Ethical conflict resolution

WHY DOES ETHICAL CONFLICT HAPPEN, AND HOW IS IT RESOLVED?

In some situations accountants will be faced with ethical conflicts. Accountants must consider how these conflicts affect their ethical principles, how these conflicts can be resolved, and the steps they must take if they cannot be resolved.

how do ethical conflicts arise?

- if the business or personal interests of an accountant affect their objectivity and independence, this creates a conflict of interest

- if the interests of two clients conflict, this also creates an ethical conflict for the accountant

- if the accountant has a conflict of loyalties between acting ethically and being loyal to their employer

organisational values and compliance with regulations

One of the ways that businesses can help to keep the risk of ethical conflict to a minimum is by ensuring that their employees comply with laws and relevant regulations.

However, organisations should also comply with 'the spirit' of the regulations, ie how these regulations are expected to work in practice.

A clear code of conduct including these key organisational values should help to do this:

■ **being transparent with colleagues, customers, and suppliers**

example: don't hide things in the small print of contracts, don't tell customers you can provide them with a product or service that is not available

effect of non-compliance: customers put off trading with the business

■ **reporting financial and regulatory information clearly and on time**

example: producing management accounts promptly and accurately for use by the business

effect of non-compliance: poor decision-making by management

- **being open and honest by identifying when it is appropriate to accept and give gifts and hospitality**

  example: only gifts worth less than £20 can only be accepted from clients, suppliers or customers

  effect of non-compliance: accusations of bribery and/or unethical behaviour

- **paying suppliers a fair price and on time**

  example: all suppliers, regardless of size, are paid on their specified credit terms

  effect of non-compliance: poor relationship with suppliers and reputational damage to the business

- **providing fair treatment, decent wages, and good working conditions for employees**

  example: provide employees with regular breaks in their working day, and suitable facilities to take their breaks

  effect of non-compliance: poor staff morale and high staff turnover

- **appropriate use of social media**

  example: clear guidance on what it is acceptable to include in social media posts

  effect of non-compliance: damage to the reputation of the business

conflict resolution

If an accountant is faced with an ethical conflict, they will need to find a method for resolving this conflict.

Larger organisations will have a **formal conflict resolution process**, which may be the best approach for the accountant to take. Alternatively, they may choose to try and **resolve the conflict informally**.

The steps an accountant should take to resolve an ethical conflict are:

- gather relevant facts relating to the conflict
- assess all the ethical issues involved
- identify the fundamental ethical principles involved in the ethical conflict
- assess whether there are established internal procedures to deal with the conflict and, if so, how they can be applied to the situation
- review alternative courses of action available
- seek advice from others

failure to resolve an ethical conflict

If the ethical conflict remains unresolved, the accountant may decide to consult with a colleague or line manager. This must be done discretely and confidentially.

If the accountant is still unable to resolve an ethical conflict, they may decide to seek further advice. This may be from:

- their employer's helpline (if the employer is big enough)

- their professional accounting body's helpline, eg AAT ethics helpline

- the person(s) responsible for governance of the business, eg the board of directors or the audit committee

- external legal advice

The accountant must always document the details of the ethical issue, together with any discussions held or decisions taken concerning this issue.

If the accountant is still unable to resolve the ethical conflict, they may have to consider stopping working on a specific project or for a particular client, or actually resigning altogether from the accountancy firm they work for or their employment.

14 Whistleblowing

IS IT TIME TO BLOW THE WHISTLE?

There are some circumstances where an individual believes that their employer, colleague, or client, has done, or is going to do, something unethical and illegal. In this situation they may feel that it is time to blow the whistle.

what is whistleblowing?

So, what do we mean by whistleblowing? A whistle blower can be defined as:

'a person who tells someone in authority about misconduct, alleged dishonesty or illegal activity that has or may occur in an organisation.'

The misconduct could be:

- breaking the law, eg bribery, fraud, or money laundering
- disregarding regulations, eg health and safety regulations, or food hygiene standards

■ doing something that is contrary to public interest, eg corruption of a local council official, or illegally dumping waste in a local river

Whistle blowers can '**speak out**' internally, ie within the organisation, or externally to regulators, or to the police.

internal whistleblowing

Internal whistleblowing involves reporting misconduct by a colleague to someone more senior in the organisation.

Doing this is a big decision which can seriously impact the individual's future employment, and in some cases may ultimately force them to resign.

what to consider when deciding to blow the whistle on a colleague

■ know all the facts surrounding the issue

■ have evidence to support the facts

■ follow the employer's internal procedures for reporting suspected misconduct, eg reporting unethical behaviour and breaches of confidentiality to a particular internal department

■ fully explain the situation to management, clearly stating the concerns and the effect on the organisation if they are not addressed

external whistleblowing

It is always advisable to raise concerns internally before taking them outside the business.

But, this is not always possible.

If an individual feels that the issue is not being addressed internally and/or the matter is **so serious** that it cannot be raised internally, the matter must be reported to an appropriate regulator such as the Financial Reporting Council (FRC), or to the police.

protection when blowing the whistle

If an employee blows the whistle on unethical or illegal behaviour by their employer, this will make it very difficult for them to continue in this employment.

So what protection is there for the employee?

The Public Interest Disclosure Act 1998 (PIDA)

PIDA protects an employee who discloses otherwise confidential information when they reasonably believe that one of the following has, or is likely to have, occurred:

- a criminal offence
- a breach of a legal obligation
- a miscarriage of justice
- endangerment of an individual's health and safety
- environmental damage

The Public Interest Disclosure Act 1998 (PIDA)

For **PIDA** to protect the employee from dismissal from their job, the employee must also be able to show that:

- they are making the disclosure in good faith

- they reasonably believe that the information disclosed is true

- they would otherwise be victimised, or the evidence concealed or destroyed, if the information is not disclosed

Although PIDA makes it easier for an employee to report an unethical or disreputable employer, it cannot offer complete protection. Inevitably, many cases of whistleblowing end up with the employee being suspended pending an enquiry or being dismissed. This may have a negative effect on their future career prospects.

seeking advice

If all else fails, an accountant may need to take external advice about how to report unethical behaviour by an employer, colleague, client, or customer.

There are several organisations that can provide confidential advice, including:

▨ Citizens Advice Bureau

▨ Protect, a charity that gives support and guidance to employees who face wrongdoing or malpractice in the workplace

▨ Professional accounting bodies. AAT has a (free) ethics helpline that is available to give advice and guidance based on the ethical code

15 Professional liability

THE RISK OF PROFESSIONAL NEGLIGENCE

If an accountant is careless in their work, or acts beyond their professional experience, knowledge, and expertise, this may be professional negligence for which they could be liable.

what is liability?

Liability means having legal responsibility for something with the possibility of having to pay damages.

Liability may arise from:

- criminal acts such as fraud or bribery
- breach of contract in the supply of services
- breach of trust
- professional negligence

Of these, the key one for an accountant is professional negligence.

In law, **negligence** is a breach of a duty of care that is implied in a particular situation or relationship.

An accountant has a duty of care to carry out assignments in a skilled and professional manner. Failure to do so would be negligent and the accountant may be liable.

professional negligence

- an accountant has a duty to exercise reasonable care and skill when they are working for a client

- if the client suffers a financial loss that they can prove is the accountant's fault, this may be considered to be **professional negligence**

- as the accountant will have entered into a contract with the client, this may also be a **breach of contract**

- if professional negligence and/or breach of contract is proved, the accountant will be **liable to pay damages** to the client

how can the risk of professional negligence be minimised?

Accountants can minimise the risk of a client suing them for professional negligence by:

■ ensuring that the exact duties included (and excluded) in the assignment are documented and agreed by the accountant and the client **before** the work starts

■ any further duties added later must also be documented and agreed

■ if an accountant does not have all the information they need from the client, they must tell the client of any limitations to their advice

■ unaudited accounts or financial statements prepared by an accountant must be clearly marked as confidential and solely for the client's use

■ for very complex assignments an accountant should take specialist advice or suggest the client does

professional indemnity insurance

No accountant wants to have a legal case for professional negligence or breach of contract brought against them by a client. But, in case it does happens, accountants in practice should ensure that they have adequate **professional indemnity insurance**.

Professional indemnity insurance is taken out to cover accountants, or other professionals, against the **legal liability** to compensate a third party (normally a client) who has suffered injury, loss, or damage through a **breach in the accountant's duty of care**.

Whilst all accountants should have professional indemnity insurance, it is **NOT** a 'safety net' in situations where an accountant does not have the necessary skills to carry out an assignment!

note: students accountants who undertake self-employed work are strongly recommended to take out professional indemnity insurance

16 Money laundering

WHAT IS MONEY LAUNDERING?

*Put simply, money laundering is moving money gained illegally, (eg terrorist funding, drug dealing, or other criminal activities) through legitimate financial systems so that the money is '**laundered**' and then appears to be '**clean**' and legally obtained.*

what are money laundering activities?

Activities related to money laundering include:

- acquiring, using, or possessing, criminal property
- handling the proceeds of crime such as theft, fraud, and tax evasion
- being knowingly involved in any way with criminal or terrorist property
- facilitating the laundering of criminal or terrorist property
- investing the proceeds of crime

- acquiring property/assets using the proceeds of crime
- transferring criminal property to another individual or business

what is criminal property?

criminal property is property knowingly obtained as a result of criminal activities eg stolen goods. It could be money, documents, tangible, or intangible property.

terrorist property is money or property likely to be used directly or indirectly for terrorist activities.

stages of money laundering

There are three stages of the process of money laundering:

PLACEMENT	LAYERING	INTEGRATION
Moving the money into a legitimate financial system. This may be by paying it into a bank account, or in more complex operations, into an offshore account. This is the stage where money laundering is most likely to be detected.	Creating a complex (layered) web of transactions to move the money around the financial system, at the same time concealing the original source and ownership of the illegal funds.	Integrating the illegal funds back into the legitimate financial system. This may be by investing in property and other assets, and will be done carefully so that the criminal creates a believable explanation of where the money has come from.

national crime agency

The National Crime Agency (**NCA**) is the law enforcement agency in the UK that is responsible for fighting serious and organised crime. As well as money laundering, the NCA investigates the supply of class A drugs, people smuggling, human trafficking, major gun crime, fraud, and computer crime.

anti-money laundering legislation in the UK

The legislation and regulations relating to money laundering in the UK, ie the anti-money laundering regime, are:

Proceeds of Crime Act 2002: sets out the principal money laundering offences and the requirements to report suspicious transactions

Terrorism Act 2000: sets out the principal terrorist financing offences and reporting obligations

Money Laundering and Terrorist Financing Regulations 2020: sets out further, more detailed, rules on money laundering

supervisory authorities in the regulated sector

Money laundering regulations apply to businesses in the regulated sector, including accountants, financial service businesses, estate agents and solicitors.

These regulated businesses must be monitored by a **supervisory authority**.

Most accountants will be supervised by their professional accounting body. If they are not, they must register with **HMRC**. Failure to do so is a criminal offence.

money laundering offences

There are three money laundering offences that may be committed by individuals or businesses. These are:

concealing – concealing (hiding), or disguising criminal property, ie what and where it is, where it came from and who owns it

arrangement – being involved in an arrangement that facilitates the acquisition, retention, use, or control, of criminal property by another person

acquisition – acquiring, using, or having possession of criminal property

It is important to note that a person does not commit these offences if they make an **authorised disclosure**, which we will cover later in this chapter.

money laundering penalties

An individual found guilty of money laundering, or the organisation that they work for, can be penalised. Dependent on the severity of the money laundering offence, this could be an **unlimited fine and/or a prison sentence of up to 14 years**.

duty to report money laundering

Accountants are required to report any suspicion that a client, employer, or colleague is involved with criminal property to the NCA in a **suspicious activity report (SAR)**.

Money Laundering Reporting Officer (MLRO) – larger organisations will have an MLRO, so any suspicion should be reported to them in an internal report.

The MLRO will review the information and decide whether to create a **SAR** and if so, report it to the NCA at the earliest opportunity.

If the accountant is a sole practitioner, they should raise the SAR themselves, and send it to the NCA.

As a minimum a SAR must contain:

- as much detail as is known about the identity of the suspected person, eg name, address, telephone numbers, passport details, date of birth, bank account details
- information on which the suspicion of money laundering is based
- location of the laundered property, if it is known
- details of who is making the report – normally the MLRO or sole practitioner

required disclosure

There are two circumstances where a **required disclosure** in an internal report or a SAR **must** be made by an accountant:

- when the accountant wishes to provide services to a client, but suspects them of money laundering or terrorist financing, they cannot work for the client until they have had consent from NCA to do so
- when the accountant actually knows or suspects money laundering or terrorist financing, regardless of whether or not they wish to act for that person. The person in question could be a client, colleague or a third party

protected disclosure

Where a required disclosure is made by **any** person, not just an accountant, this is a **protected disclosure**.

This means they are protected against any allegations of **breaching confidentiality**.

authorised disclosure

Any person, not just an accountant, who realises that **they** may have engaged or are about to engage in money laundering, should make an **authorised disclosure** to the appropriate authority.

The disclosure should be made before the act is carried out, or if this is not possible, as soon after the act has happened.

Making an authorised disclosure may provide the person with a defence against charges of money laundering against them.

failure to disclose

It is an offence for an accountant not to report their suspicion of money laundering.

Failure to disclose carries a maximum penalty of **five years imprisonment and/or a fine**.

An accountant who fails to disclose their suspicion may face **disciplinary action** by their professional accounting body, eg AAT.

prejudicing an investigation

Any person who knows or suspects that a money laundering investigation is being conducted or might be conducted and either says or does something that is likely to prejudice the investigation, or falsifies, conceals, or destroys documents relating to the investigation, may be **prejudicing an investigation**.

The offence may apply even if they did not intend to prejudice an investigation.

The maximum penalty for prejudicing an investigation is **five years imprisonment and/or a fine**.

tipping off

If an accountant thinks or knows a report of money laundering has been made to the MLRO, the NCA, HMRC's fraud hotline, or the police, and then warns the person suspected, this is **tipping off**.

The person who tips off the suspect can be prosecuted for this money laundering offence, even if they didn't mean to prejudice the investigation.

The maximum penalty for tipping off is **five years imprisonment and/or a fine**.

Although tipping off is an offence, an accountant is entitled to advise their clients in general terms about the issue of money laundering.

exceptions to the duty to report money laundering

Accountants are **not** obliged to report suspicions of money laundering if:

- their suspicion is basis on information obtained outside the accountant's work, for example during a social occasion
- their suspicion resulted from privileged circumstances, eg if an accountant found out about possible money laundering when giving a client's advice about their tax liability. However, the accountant must be careful not to give the client advice on how to commit a criminal offence and/or avoid detection, eg tax evasion
- there is a reasonable excuse for not reporting immediately (this is very unlikely as a reasonable excuse has never been defined)

WHAT IMPACT DOES TECHNOLOGY HAVE ON ACCOUNTING SYSTEMS?

Emerging and developing technologies including automation, artificial intelligence (AI), machine learning, blockchain, electronic filing and signing of documents, and data analytics, will all have a significant impact on the way accounting systems operate.

what are the benefits of automating accounting processes?

- **automate essential accounting tasks** – software can be used to carry out repetitive tasks, eg sending out customer statements, reconciling accounts, updating financial records, or creating financial statements

- **improved data integrity** – because the software does the work, the chance of human error is reduced

- **more efficient approval** – management approval can be done more quickly if the software automatically sends documents to the appropriate person
- **greater internal data visibility** – easy access to data means the business can promptly identify what is working, and any issues that might need to be addressed
- **quicker payment from customers** – if the software generates invoices and statements promptly, this will result in quicker receipt of payment

Accountants should not see automation as a threat as it can never replace humans completely.

Using automated processes means that, increasingly, the accountant's role will be less a 'number cruncher' and more a business advisor.

artificial intelligence (AI) and machine learning

AI is a computer system that is able to simulate the way that humans think and behave. The computer processes and analyses large volumes of data to work out how it is dealt with by humans. Once enough 'intelligence' has been gained, it treats the data in the same way.

This sounds a bit 'sci-fi', but in fact, AI is increasingly being used by businesses in their day-to-day operations.

machine learning uses AI to code computers to learn from data, without being programmed to do every task. It uses past events to predict what will happen next, eg Amazon will target customers with specific advertising, based on their viewing history that it has 'learnt'.

So, how can AI and machine learning be used in the accounting system?

There are many uses, including:

- **automatic coding** – the system will know how to automatically post financial documents, including sales and purchases invoices, payments and receipts, leading to accurate and prompt reporting

- **audit of information** – the software can review large amounts of data quickly, and highlight any 'unusual' items that need to be investigated
- **forecasting** – AI can be used to predict (forecast) future events, eg price changes or movements in exchange rates
- **analysing complex data** – bespoke AI and machine learning can be used to carry out analysis, which would otherwise require specialist financial staff

but.....

- development costs, and ongoing running costs, for these systems are expensive, and they will need to be updated regularly as technology changes
- accountants may be reluctant to embrace the new technology, with mistrust and fear of redundancy being key factors

blockchain

Blockchain is a digital ledger of transactions that is shared across the entire network of computers in the particular blockchain.

Information is duplicated and shared across a huge number of users in the blockchain, stopping records from being altered, deleted, or destroyed.

the creation of a blockchain transaction step-by-step

1 user raises a transaction

2 block is created digitally representing the transaction

3 block is distributed to **every** computer in the blockchain

4 **every** computer validates the transaction to prove it is authentic

5 complete, authenticated block is added to the chain

But **why**?

Blockchain can protect against data hacking because of the following features:

■ each transaction is shared across the internet by all users in the blockchain

- **all** the details of the transaction are recorded by **all** the users in the blockchain eg amount, date, time, location, bank name, account number, of a bank deposit

- ledgers of all users in the blockchain will be updated for all transactions, but only when they have **all** agreed it is consistent. This prevents a single system adding new unauthorised blocks to the chain

- each new block added is linked to the previous one using a cryptographic hash, which encrypts the data so only authorised users have access

- any attempt to manipulate the data by an unauthorised user will be rejected

how is blockchain useful in accounting systems?

- provides certainty about the ownership of assets

- maintains ledgers of accurate information

- improves data security

- takes on recordkeeping so that accounting staff can carry out other work

electronic document filing

Electronic file management systems, where files are held on a computer server or in 'the cloud', have a number of **benefits**:

- instant access to any authorised user in any location at any time
- reduced need for multiple copies of documents
- files are better organised
- improved version control as there is a full document history
- automatic back up protects files against natural disasters, eg fire or flood
- improved productivity as files are more easily accessed

However, there are some **disadvantages** of this method of filing:

- filing software will need to be kept up-to-date
- significant initial cost to set up the system
- risk of data breaches

electronic document signing

There are several ways documents can be signed electronically.

simple electronic signatures eg scanning a physical signature or prepopulated form with a box where a signature can automatically generate. This can be used by individuals but not organisations

advanced electronic signatures – electronic identifier uniquely linked to the signatory, eg app on their phone that validates their signature

qualified electronic signatures – electronically witnessing the signature by a third-party trust service provider (TSP) provides additional security

Electronic signing is a useful tool for the finance function as it speeds up document processing, but care must be taken if a legally enforceable method of signing is needed.

data analytics

This is collecting, organising, and analysing large amounts of data that a business has gathered internally and externally.

The four types of data analytics are:

■ **descriptive** **what has happened?** Data analytics that look at, and then report on, past performance.

example: monthly sales report by branch

■ **diagnostic** **why did it happen?** Detailed analysis of the causes of what has happened.

example: why product sales have fluctuated month on month

■ **predictive** **what is likely to happen next?** Uses large volumes of data to predict (forecast) what is likely to happen in the future – like human forecasting, it can never be 100% accurate.

example: daily sales in supermarkets to estimate how much of each product to deliver to each location

■ **prescriptive**   **what action needs to be taken?** Uses a combination of machine
learning, algorithms (complex mathematical tools) and rules set by
the business, to make recommendations of action to be taken

*example: analysing sales of all products in all supermarket
locations to decide what to continue to stock where*

usefulness of data analytics

■ handles large volumes of data quickly, which speeds up reporting processes and
decision-making

■ can reduce the risk of fraud by identifying inconsistencies in information and working
out how they may have happened

■ helps the business to focus its activities, either because they are already profitable, or
because it has identified trends indicating which products will be popular in the future

Predictive and prescriptive data analytics, in particular, can be expensive, so businesses
need to assess their benefit before using them.

outsourcing and technology

Developments in technology have allowed businesses to **outsource** to a third party certain tasks, provision of services, or handling of operations, that the business has previously done in-house.

examples of outsourcing are:

- manufacturing processes

- human resources tasks

- finance functions, eg bookkeeping and payroll

- legal services

- facilities management

- catering

- cleaning

advantages of outsourcing

- cost savings – fewer staff means lower wages and training costs, and capital expenditure will reduce. However, this change in cost structure will mean that, whilst capital costs reduce, expenses increase

- staff time made available to carry out core operations

- expertise of the outsourcing business

- no longer required to comply with certain regulations and legislation

disadvantages of outsourcing

- loss of expertise if core operations are outsourced

- quality issues due to outsourcing business not having the same levels of skill

- difficult to move the work back in-house at a later date

- data security, eg product designs, or confidential data such as payroll records

- adverse effect on staff morale if outsourcing results in redundancies

- future cost increases from the outsourcing business once the business is reliant on it

- disruption in supply if there are issues at the outsourcing business

offshoring and technology

This is when organisations relocate some of their operations to another country. Improved technology allows high quality, instant and reliable communication across the world, making offshoring much easier for businesses.

Offshoring is normally done by businesses in developed countries to less developed countries, with the main purpose being to reduce cost.

examples of offshoring are:

■ data processing

■ manufacturing, eg in the clothing industry

■ call centres

advantages of offshoring	disadvantages of offshoring
• cost savings • higher visibility in the overseas country • availability of staff 24/7 due to time differences • wider pool of expertise available	• cultural and language barriers • complicated legal and tax implications eg payroll • exchange rate changes may affect costs • implications for corporate social responsibility eg overseas working conditions and rates of pay

18 Cloud accounting

WHY HAVE AN ACCOUNTING SYSTEM IN THE CLOUD?

Developments in technology mean that many businesses now store their data in 'the cloud'. Cloud computing means that data and resources are stored on remote servers, allowing 'on demand' access. Examples are iCloud and Google Drive.

Data is up-to-date and can be accessed from any compatible device and shared with other users with access authority.

what is cloud accounting?

Cloud accounting software moves the whole accounting process to the cloud, with information stored on remote, secure servers, owned by the cloud accounting system provider. Users subscribe to the system and all their accounting records will be held in the cloud.

Cloud accounting systems have become more popular in recent years – examples are Quickbooks and Xero.

key features of cloud accounting

- **remote access** – users can access the software from anywhere with the internet

- **remote data storage** – data is automatically backed up to the cloud each time a new piece of data is added

- **shared access** – cloud accounting allows all parts of the organisation to see the same information at the same time

- **multi-user access** – several individuals can use data at the same time

- **automation capabilities** – some cloud accounting systems incorporate some AI and machine learning that recognise and automatically post transactions

- **availability of apps/plug-ins/add-ins** – apps allow access to the system from tablets or phones. Plug-ins and add-ins allow users to customise reports to fit with the business's needs

- **interaction with stakeholders** – the business can communicate financial information quickly and efficiently to stakeholders in user-friendly formats, eg dashboards

- **real-time data** – data is always up-to-date

further benefits of cloud accounting

In addition to the features of cloud accounting above, further benefits include:

- **lower IT costs** – the business has no costs of buying and maintaining a server, reduced costs of IT expertise, and no back-up processes are required

- **improved sustainability** – cloud accounting means less printing and paper are used as things can be generated and sent automatically

- **better security** – cloud accounting software companies will use a data centre, with sophisticated levels of security to protect both the software and the data

disadvantages of cloud accounting

- **reliance on internet access** – users will only be able to access the computer accounting system if they have a strong, stable internet connection

- **software requirements** – all stakeholders need to have the same cloud accounting software installed on their computers or devices, which will need to be kept up-to-date

- **switching may be difficult** – once a business is using a particular cloud accounting software, it may be difficult to then switch to an alternative system in the future

19 Data protection, information security and cybersecurity

KEEPING INFORMATION SECURE

Businesses that hold personal data must adhere to the key data protection principles included in the Data Protection Act 2018 and GDPR.

Businesses must also have appropriate controls in place, including cybersecurity, to protect their systems and data against the risk of cyberattacks.

principles of data protection

As part of their operations, businesses collect a large amount of personal data about individuals, including employees and customers. **The Data Protection Act 2018** incorporates the requirements of the EU General Data Protection Regulation (**GDPR**).

The key data protection principles are set out over the next two pages.

Data protection principles

lawfulness, fairness, and transparency	when an organisation processes personal data it must be **for a good reason**, and the business should be open and honest about what these reasons are
purpose limitation	personal data should only be used for the **explicit purpose** for which it was given
data minimisation	organisations should **collect the minimum** amount of personal data that is necessary for the specific purpose
accuracy	organisations that collect personal data must ensure that the **data is accurate, and that it is kept up-to-date**

storage limitation	personal data held by an organisation must not be kept any longer than necessary and it should be able to justify how long it holds on to the data
integrity and confidentiality	personal data must be kept secure from internal and external threats, and protected from unauthorised access, unlawful processing, accidental loss, destruction, or damage
accountability	an organisation must have appropriate measures and records to prove it complies with data processing principles, as supervisory authorities can ask for this evidence at any time

breaches in data protection

- data protection breaches may occur due to:
  - errors made by those handling the data
  - deliberate, criminal attacks

- Information Commissioner's Office (**ICO**) regulates and enforces GDPR in the UK

- **maximum fine** for a data protection breach in the **UK** is the greater of £17.5 million (€20 million in the **EU**), or 4% of annual global turnover

- personal data breaches must be reported to the relevant supervisory body within 72 hours, and if there is a high risk of it adversely affecting an individual's rights and freedoms, they must be informed immediately

- organisations must have robust data breach detection, investigation, and internal reporting procedures in place to allow them to decide who to notify of a breach

- organisations must keep a record of all personal data breaches

maintaining information security

To maintain information security and minimise the risk of data breaches, organisations must implement certain controls.

accounting systems access levels	**passwords** restricting access to certain parts of the system, eg payroll
	electronic access logs that keep a record of who has accessed different areas of the system and the data
security controls	**firewalls** are security devices that sit between an organisation's internal network and the public internet. They are designed to **let in** non-threatening traffic, but **keep out** dangerous traffic, ie hackers and viruses

integrity controls (over the accuracy and completeness of data)	**input controls** provide reasonable assurance that transactions are complete and have been properly authorised before being processed
	eg sequence checking and reconciling batch totals
	processing controls ensure data is processed properly, or to prevent more than one user updating the same data record at the same time
	eg matching of two, or more, items before processing, such as invoice to goods received note
	output controls ensure the integrity of data output from the system. This may be by reconciling data in the system, or a system user reviewing it and signing it off
	eg reconciling the payables control account to the payables ledger, or reviewing the BACS supplier payment schedule before submission to the bank for payment

cyber risk

The increased use of technology has meant that for most businesses **cyber risk** has increased.

Cyber risk is any risk associated with financial loss, disruption, or reputational damage from unauthorised use of its information systems.

cyberattacks

A cyberattack is a malicious and deliberate attempt by someone outside the organisation to access its information. It is often done for the attacker's financial benefit, although sometimes the attack may simply intend to disrupt the business.

Key examples of cyberattacks are:

phishing   attacker sends a message to someone within the organisation trying to trick them into opening the email or an attachment. If opened, this will release malware into the system, or will identify information in the system that allows the attacker to access its network and data

malware	software inserted into computers via phishing emails, links, or attachments. It attempts to introduce viruses, worms, or ransomware into the organisation's network which then multiply and spread across the system ultimately stopping it from operating
ransomware	malware that locks a user out of their own information systems before asking them to pay a 'ransom'. If this is not paid, the attacker may release the organisation's confidential data online
denial-of-service attack (DDoS)	overwhelms the organisation's central server with huge numbers of data requests at the same time, causing the system to freeze up until the attacker's demands are met
spyware	virus that gets into an organisation's system and allows the attacker to spy on its operations without been seen
keylogging	records every keystroke made by a user, and then recreates them to identify passwords and other sensitive information

cybersecurity

A cyberattack may cause:

▓ **loss of data**	relating to customers, suppliers, or employees
▓ **disruption to business operations**	due to IT failure caused by malware or cyber attacks

Cybersecurity that businesses use to protect systems from cyberattacks include:

▓ **firewalls** (see page 154)

▓ **antivirus software** runs in the background providing protection against virus attacks by scanning, detecting, and deleting viruses from a system in real-time

▓ **data encryption software** that translates data into another form, or code, so that only authorised users with a 'decryption key', or password, can read it. It protects confidential data that is stored or transmitted electronically

20 Good quality information

GOOD QUALITY INFORMATION AND WHO USES IT

*The attributes of good quality information can be remembered using the acronym **ACCURATE**. But as well as providing good quality information, it is important to provide the right information to different levels of the business, ie strategic, managerial, and operational levels.*

what is the difference between data and information?

data	information
raw facts and figures	data that has been processed so that it is organised, structured, and well presented, making it useful and meaningful for the user

attributes of good quality information

The attributes of good quality information can be remembered using the acronym **ACCURATE**.

A ccurate	information should be free from errors, free from bias, and sufficiently accurate to be relied upon
C omplete	sufficient information for the purpose it is required for, with nothing missing, but not excessive
C ost effective	the cost of producing the information should not be greater than its value and usefulness
U nderstandable	the style, format, detail, and complexity of information should fit the user's needs, ie user-targeted
R elevant	information should be fit for purpose, and communicated to the right person, ie whoever is using it to plan
A uthoritative	information should come from a reliable source. This may be the person who provides it, or the computer program that produces it
T imely	information should be communicated in sufficient time for the user to make the necessary decisions
E asy to use	information should be provided in a way that makes it easy to use

different management levels in an organisation

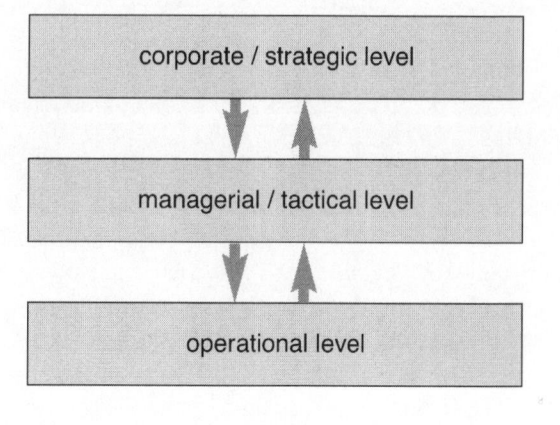

information at strategic/corporate level

■ **highest level** of the organisation where strategic decisions are made

■ **planning the future** direction of the business and setting goals

■ bases **longer-term** decisions on past information, eg revenue growth targets based on previous years' growth

■ focuses more heavily on **external information** that affects the business, eg competitor activities, government policies, interest rates, exchange rates or inflation

■ information will be **summarised** rather than detailed – lower levels of management will carry out the analysis before it is presented to strategic management

■ information is likely to be required on an **ad-hoc** rather than a regular basis

information at managerial level

■ **middle level** of management where decisions about how to achieve strategic goals will be made

■ translates the strategic vision into a **practical, tactical** plan

■ relies on **regular**, operational information to monitor progress towards the organisation's goals

■ information required will mostly be generated **internally**

■ information needs to be **sufficiently detailed** for planning and allocation of resources

information at operational level

- **lowest level** of management that is involved in the day-to-day running of the business

- required to **implement strategic and tactical decisions** made at the higher management levels

- requires **explicit, detailed information** to make immediate decisions

- information required will be **regular** and **detailed** from **internal sources**

- information generally to relate to **past events**

21 Big data

WHAT MAKES DATA BIG AND WHY IS IT USEFUL?

Big data can be defined as a collection of data which is so large and complex, and which accumulates so quickly, that it is difficult to store and process using traditional data processing software.

But what are the characteristics of big data, and how can a business benefit from collecting, processing, and managing it?

sources of internal and external big data

Three primary sources of big data are:

social data   comes from social media and gives organisations invaluable insight into the ways customers think and behave so they can focus their products and marketing

examples: tweets (and retweets) on Twitter, and likes and comments on Facebook and Instagram

machine data	generated by all kind of machines and generally well-structured and easier to analyse
	examples: sensors in medical equipment, handheld scanners used by delivery couriers, checkout scanners in supermarkets combined with loyalty cards, electricity smart meters, and online computer games played via the internet
transactional data	generated from the daily transactions of a business – it includes huge amounts of data about every individual transaction, including information about customers
	examples: details about suppliers, products, prices, locations, and importantly, the links between each of these and all the data included in the sales and purchases, payments and receipts, and other transactions of the business

characteristics of big data

The characteristics of big data are often referred to as '**the five Vs**'.

Volume   the size and amount of data that businesses manage and analyse

Velocity   the speed (velocity) at which businesses receive and process data

Variety   the diversity and range of different types and sources of data

Veracity   how accurate, or truthful, the data is – high volumes of the data, and the speed it is being generated, increases the risk of inaccuracies, or bias, so data must be obtained from a trusted source

Value   the value of big data comes from the insight it gives to businesses, leading to more effective operation of the business, and better customer relationships

benefits of using big data

Benefits of collecting, processing, and managing big data include:

- **attracting and retaining customers** – identifying patterns in behaviour and suggesting products the customer may like

- **focused marketing** – analysing trends to focus marketing

- **gain competitive advantage** – analysing big data effectively will provide an advantage over competitors in the same market

- **identifying areas of potential risk** – analysing big data identifies riskier areas in the business and allows prompt action before the risk becomes too great

- **faster innovation** – collection and analysis of big data means the business can quickly react to changes in tastes and market trends

- **improved business processes** – analysis of big data means the business can streamline its operations to improve processes which will help it to control costs

- **fraud detection** – machine learning technology means banks and other financial institutions can detect fraudulent transactions more easily

limitations and risks of using big data

■ **lack of knowledge and skills** – there are two issues here: insufficient skilled professionals to analyse data and those that are available are expensive, and a lack of ongoing training to ensure their skills and knowledge remain up-to-date

■ **difficulties integrating data from different sources** – the wide variety of data formats available may overwhelm data analysis tools and result in incomplete and/or inaccurate information

■ **data protection** – businesses must ensure they adhere to the data protection principles covered in Chapter 19, when holding and processing such large volumes of data

■ **data security** – businesses must ensure they have sufficient resource to protect the data against the risks of data leaks, hacking or data losses

applying professional scepticism in relation to big data

In Chapter 11 we saw that **professional scepticism** is an attitude that includes:

■ a questioning mind, ie not taking what is said at face value

- being alert to the possibility of misstatement due to error or fraud, and using professional experience to identify signs of genuine errors or deliberate fraud

- critically assessing evidence that is provided

Professional scepticism must be applied before big data is used as the basis of key business decisions. It is not acceptable to simply assume that because it's been analysed 'it must be right'.

data analytics from external sources

Some businesses will use professional data analytics companies with the specialist skills to provide analysis. This will reduce costs but there are some **drawbacks**:

- external analytics companies may not have specialist knowledge of the business sector in which the organisation operates

- the business must rely on the professional analysts to maintain the security of the data and comply with the data protection principles covered in Chapter 19

22 Visualising information

PRESENTING INFORMATION VISUALLY

Data visualisation is a good way of making financial, and non-financial, information understandable for non-financial managers and staff. Information can be presented as images, diagrams, graphs, tables, matrices, and charts in an accessible and usable way by summarising and simplifying large amounts of complex information.

different formats for visualising information

This section will detail some of the formats that are commonly used by businesses to present information.

tables

Tables are one of the simplest ways of presenting information and are often generated using spreadsheet software.

Quarterly sales by division (£000)					
	Quarter 1	**Quarter 2**	**Quarter 3**	**Quarter 4**	**Total**
	£000	£000	£000	£000	£000
Scotland	421	479	512	410	**1,822**
North	745	711	645	722	**2,823**
Midlands	1,121	1,041	1,245	924	**4,331**
South	1,274	1,144	1,578	1,431	**5,427**
Total	3,561	3,375	3,980	3,487	**14,403**

advantages of tables

- clear presentation
- easy to compare figures
- patterns can be identified
- abnormalities can be identified
- easy to prepare and understand

disadvantages of tables

- too much data can overwhelm the user
- data may get lost in a very large table
- information is limited to being shown in two dimensions, ie rows and columns

matrices

A **matrix** is a simplified table that uses colours, icons, or pictures rather than actual figures, making it easier to understand. The matrix in the example below uses the same information from the table in the previous section using a hollow spot to represent the lowest sales in each quarter, and a filled spot for the highest.

Quarterly sales by division				
	Quarter 1	**Quarter 2**	**Quarter 3**	**Quarter 4**
Scotland			●	○
North	●		○	
Midlands			●	○
South		○	●	

advantages of matrices

- key data stands out

- visually appealing to less numerate users

disadvantage of matrices

- lack of detail

- only useful where a focused message is required

column and bar charts

The height of the columns, or the length of the bars, represent the value of each item.

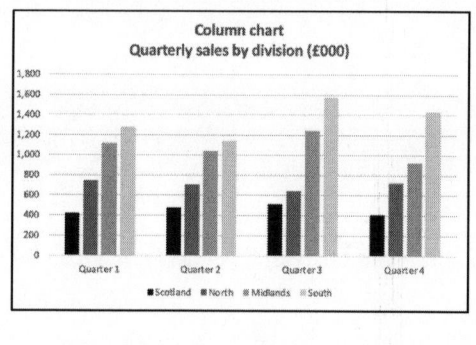

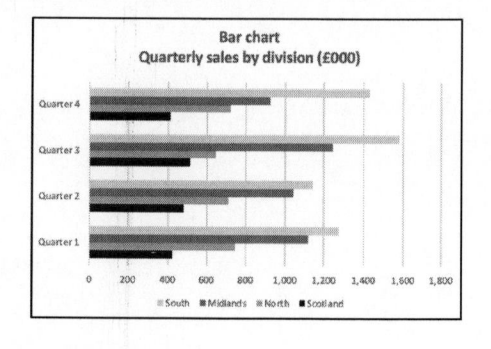

- useful where several sets of data are being compared
- too many bars or columns may make it difficult to interpret

- can be made visually clearer by making them three dimensional (3D) like the one below

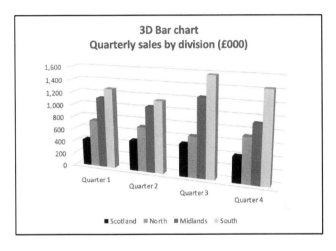

pie charts

A **pie chart** is a circle divided into sections to represent the proportion each part makes up of the whole – like a pie divided into slices.

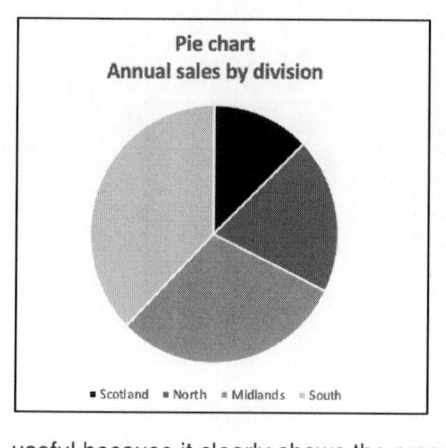

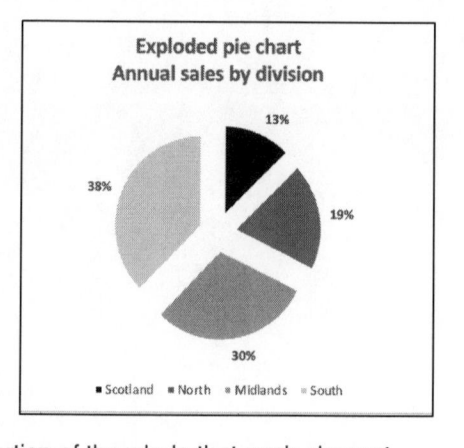

■ useful because it clearly shows the proportion of the whole that each element represents

For variety, pie charts can also be shown as a doughnut.

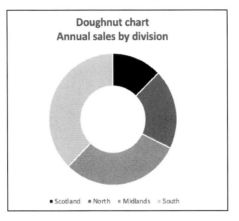

line graphs

A line graph plots continuous data, clearly showing trends.

If the line graph shows two related sets of figures, eg sales and costs, the gap between the two lines (in this case, profit) is also clearly represented to the user.

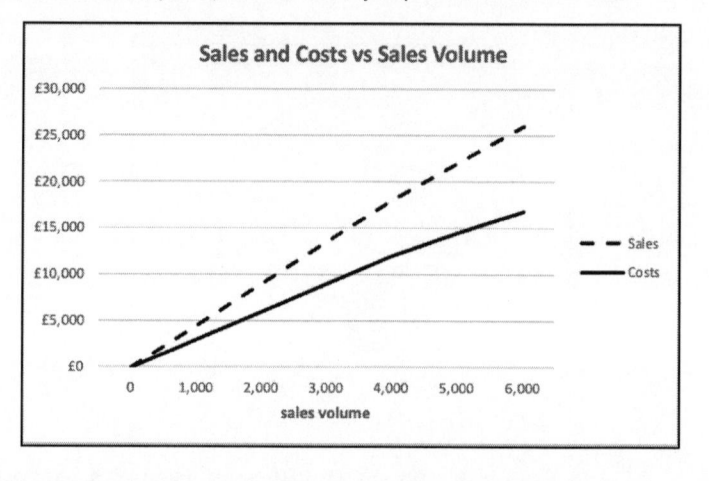

diagrams

A **diagram** helps the user to see relationships between information.

Diagrams are particularly good to show movement of information through a process and make a more visual impact than a simple description or calculation.

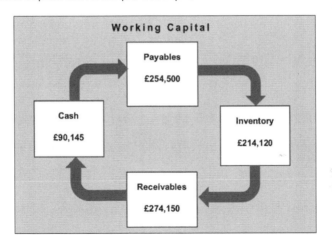

images

An **image** is a picture or photograph.

- not widely used in data visualisation
- a photograph will reinforce the message it is trying to put across
- images sometimes used to support figures and increase their impact
- particularly useful to where the users do not have a specialist knowledge of the data

what type of data visualisation should be used?

This will depend on three questions.

WHO is it for?

examples: *a strategic level presentation, eg to directors, may use graphs and charts that clearly show trends*

                  detailed sales information required by the sales manager might be better presented in a table

WHAT type of data is it?

examples: *trends in monthly sales over a 12-month period presented to the sales teams would be presented using a line graph*

                  the split of total sales by product could be clearly presented using a pie chart

HOW will the data be presented?

examples: *graphs and charts can be explained as part of a presentation*

                  tables with written analysis and explanation would be better in a report

PRESENTING INFORMATION VISUALLY

Dashboards form part of computerised accounting software and are helpful for managers and owners of organisations that do not have a financial background. They present data visually using graphs, charts, diagrams, and tables summarising relevant information on one page, and making it easier to understand.

benefits of a dashboard

- data is easy to understand and in sufficient detail for many smaller businesses, even if the owner does not have a financial background

- dashboards can be customised to present information so that it is relevant

- the dashboard can be produced in real-time as required, and is always up-to-date

- if the dashboard is part of a cloud-based accounting system, it can be accessed from any device and any location with internet access

example of a computer accounting dashboard

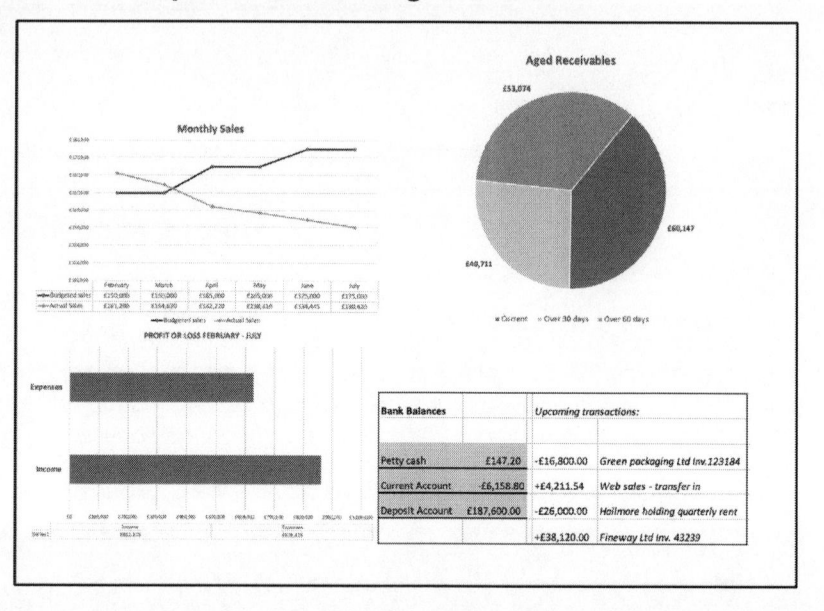

interpreting the dashboard

Users must be able to **interpret** what the dashboard is telling them, so the dashboard should allow the user to see relationships between different sets of information and **identify trends**.

In the assessment for this unit you will need to be able to review a dashboard and use the information it shows, together with details of the business's operations, to identify and assess trends and relationships between figures and make suggestions for action that can be take.

In this example:

▓ sales above budget for February and March, but from April onwards, sales decreased month-on-month. If sales continue to fall compared with budget, the business may have a cash flow issue. The business should increase marketing

▓ consider transferring some of the funds from the deposit account to the overdrawn current account as the upcoming transactions mean it may go more overdrawn

▓ a significant proportion of the total aged receivables are more than 60 days overdue. Credit control procedures should be tightened up to ensure that customers pay more promptly

▓ the deterioration in sales compared with budget and the high level of overdue receivables may cause reduced profit and cash flow in the future

EFFECTIVE COMMUNICATION

Communication must be clear and easily understood, concise, unambiguous, complete, accurate, and provided at the right time and in the most appropriate format, to ensure the smooth flow of ideas, facts, decision-making, and advice.

effective communication

Communication in the workplace can be internal, eg with other staff members, or external, eg with suppliers or customers. Whoever the communication is with, it must be effective.

Effective, professional communication should have the following attributes:

- **clear** and easily understood
- **concise** – no unnecessary information
- **unambiguous** – avoid technical language, or anything that is misleading
- **complete** – include everything that is needed
- **accurate**
- **timely** – provided on time
- **appropriate** – meets the needs whoever the communication is with
- in the most **suitable format**

methods of communication

You will have learned about the methods of communication at level 2 and the fact that they can be written, verbal or electronic.

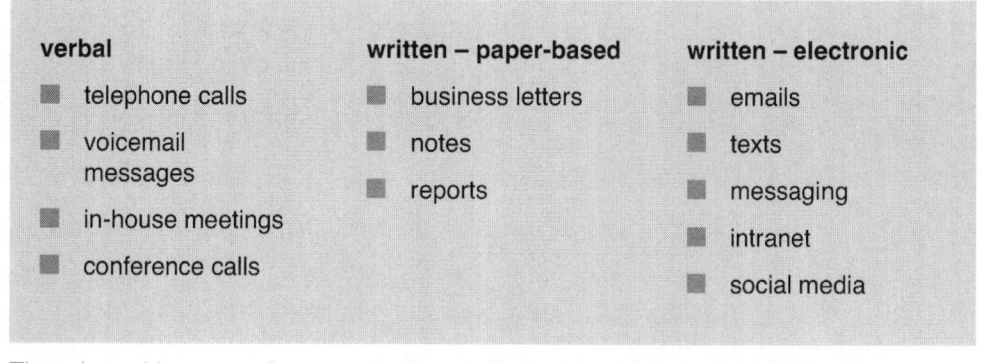

verbal

- telephone calls
- voicemail messages
- in-house meetings
- conference calls

written – paper-based

- business letters
- notes
- reports

written – electronic

- emails
- texts
- messaging
- intranet
- social media

There is a wide range of communication methods, but which one is right for different circumstances? Over the next few pages we will look at the characteristics and uses of some of the main communication methods used by businesses.

Whichever method of communication is used, it is important to ensure that **confidentiality** is maintained where necessary.

report

- used to communicate information on a **specific subject** to individuals, or groups of individuals

- **routine reports** may be produced regularly, eg a weekly aged receivables report produced by the credit controller that includes analysis and explanation, or as a **one-off report** at the request of a particular user

- reports should follow a **clear structure** including a summary, introduction, findings, conclusion, and recommendations. Detailed figures supporting the report should be included in an appendix

- reports are, primarily, used to communicate with internal stakeholders, eg managers and directors

- one-off report for external stakeholders might include a report to support a bank loan application, or a corporate social responsibility (CSR) report

email

- **most common way of communicating** in a business environment

- quick and efficient way of communicating

- can include an electronic 'signature', with the sender's name, job title, business name, and the sender's contact details

- should be professional and avoid slang, emojis, or exclamation marks

- attachments can be added to emails which is useful to transfer documents

- email systems can have an encryption function to protect confidentiality

- emails can be used to communicate internally and externally

- emails are routinely used for internal communication between colleagues

- emails can be used to communicate with suppliers and customers, including sending documents such as invoices, statements, or credit control letters

letter

- where more **formal communication** is required, businesses may use a letter

- a business letter should use the organisation's '**house style**' ie the look and format of each letter is in a uniform style, on standard printed stationery that shows all the details of the business

- letters are **normally used for external communication**, eg a bank or solicitor

- internal communication by letter is limited to formal situations, eg when a member of staff receives a promotion, or where their employment is terminated

telephone call

- **quick** way of communicating, used internally by staff to confirm arrangements, raising, or resolving queries, or discussing issues

- increasingly, telephone calls are made across the internet with cameras on, so they are more like a meeting

- telephone calls can also be used externally to contact external stakeholders, eg if requested by a customer or supplier, or if a verbal discussion is required

meeting

- meetings can be held in person, or over the internet using Zoom, Microsoft Teams, Skype, or Google Hangouts, etc

- can be formal or informal

- can be between two, or more, people

- internal meetings include team meetings, project meetings, management meetings, and board meetings

- external meetings can be with customers, suppliers, the bank, or sometimes with the general public, eg where planning permission is being sought

- should be well structured, with an agenda

- everyone who is attending should be able to contribute during the meeting

- individuals attending the meeting must be aware of non-verbal signs, or body language, during a meeting. Positive, non-verbal signals include nodding and smiling, negative signals include frowning, lack of eye contact or tone of voice

intranet and instant messaging

- an intranet is a **secure, private network** that is used for sharing information and accessing and sharing files internally

- allows secure communication, back up of data, and data security in business

- an organisation's intranet can have a chat function allowing easy and quick internal communication via instant messaging

social media

- most businesses use social media, eg Twitter, Instagram, or Facebook

- uses include attracting new customers, engaging with existing customers, or promoting CSR

- content must be appropriate, and not cause offensive as this could adversely affect the reputation of the business

- businesses should have rules and guidance on the use of social media, with all content reviewed and approved before it is posted

25 Memory aids

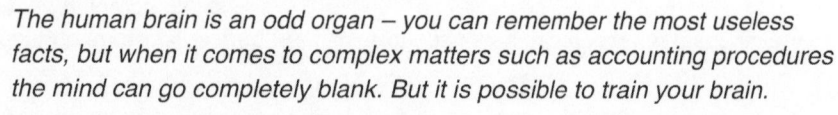

KEEPING YOUR MEMORY FIT

The human brain is an odd organ – you can remember the most useless facts, but when it comes to complex matters such as accounting procedures the mind can go completely blank. But it is possible to train your brain.

At the beginning of this Guide there are some revision tips which suggest that you can study effectively and recall information by . . .

■ ***Observing**, ie remembering what information looks like on the page, using diagrams, lists, mind-maps and colour coding. Memory is very visual.*

■ ***Writing** information down, using flash cards, post-it notes, notes on a phone. It is the actual process of writing which helps to fix the information in the brain.*

■ ***Learning** by regularly going through your course notes and text books. Find a 'study buddy' in your class (or online) to teach and test each other as the course progresses.*

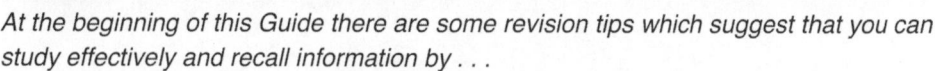

■ **Chill out** when you get tired. Give your brain a chance to recover. Get some exercise and fresh air, work out. In the ancient world there was the saying that "a fit body is home to a fit mind."

■ **Treats** – promise yourself rewards when you have finished studying – meet friends, eat chocolate, have a drink, listen to music.

exam preparation

■ **Practice, practice, practice** when preparing for your assessment.

Practice the questions and assessments in the Osborne Books workbooks.

Practice the free online assessments on the Osborne Books website by visiting www.osbornebooks.co.uk/elearning

using memory aids

On the next few pages are blank spaces for you to set out some of the important words and phrases you may need to for your assessment.

1 RISK

List the four actions to address risk identified by the TARA framework
T
A
R
A

2 PESTLE

List the six factors that make up a PESTLE analysis
P
E
S
T
L
E

3 MICRO-ECONOMIC ENVIRONMENT

What is meant by each of the following?
Normal good
Inferior good
Necessity good
Substitute good
Complementary good

4 ETHICAL PRINCIPLES AND THREATS

List the five fundamental ethical principles	List the five categories of threat to the fundamental ethical principles
■	■
■	■
■	■
■	■
■	■

5 DATA PROTECTION PRINCIPLES

List the seven data protection principles
■
■
■
■
■
■
■

6 GOOD QUALITY INFORMATION

What does the mnemonic ACCURATE stand for?
A
C
C
U
R
A
T
E

7 THE FIVE Vs OF BIG DATA

List the five characteristics of big data
V
V
V
V
V

index